MR. LEVINE AND ME

Stories to Remember for the Rest of Your Life

MR. LEVINE AND ME

Stories to Remember for
the Rest of Your Life
Rabbi Michael Weisser

SENTIENT PUBLICATIONS

First Sentient Publications edition 2025

Copyright © 2025 by Deborah Weisser

All rights reserved. This book, or parts thereof, may not be reproduced in any form without permission, except in the case of brief quotations embodied in critical articles and reviews.

A paperback original

Book design by Laura Johanna Waltje
Cover Design by Laura Johanna Waltje
Cover photo courtesy of Colin M. Caplan

Library of Congress Control Number: 2024949578
Publisher's Cataloging-in-Publication Data

Names: Weisser, Michael, author.

Title: Mr. Levine and me : stories to remember for the rest of your life / Rabbi Michael Weisser.

Description: Boulder, CO: Sentient Publications, 2025.

Identifiers: LCCN: 2024949578 | ISBN: 978-1-59181-326-2 (paperback) | 978-1-59181-327-9 (epub)

Subjects: LCSH Weisser, Micheal. | New Haven (Conn.)--Biography. | New Haven Region (Conn.)--Social life and customs--20th century. | Jews--Connecticut--New Haven--Biography. | BISAC Biography & Autobiography / Personal Memoirs | Self-Help / Motivational & Inspirational
Classification: LCC F104.N653 .W 2025 | DDC 974.67/092--dc23

SENTIENT PUBLICATIONS
A Limited Liability Company
PO Box 1851
Boulder, CO 80306
www.sentientpublications.com

Contents

Prologue	1
Growing up on the Avenue	3
Mr. Levine	8
Never Take the Rap for the Other Guy	12
You Are Who You Are	19
You Know What You Get from Wanting?	22
The Truth Will Win	28
Brothers and Friends	32
Very Perfect	37
An Aside	41
If Somebody Needs Your Help, Help Them	45
Whatever You Do Has Your Name on It	49
It Doesn't Matter Who the Other Guy Is.	54
Your Life Is the Only Story You Get to Tell	57
Nobody Can Make You Happy	61
If You Hide Who You Are, You're Nobody	66
Spend Some, Save Some, Give Some Away	71
Being Afraid Sometimes Is a Good Thing	74
Never Say I Love You Unless You Know What You're Talking About	79
If You Succeed at Something, Try Something Harder	86
Today, I Am a Man	89
Ochi Chernye: Dark Eyes	94
Learn to Bake Bread	100
Dmitro, I'm Gonna Tell You Something	103
Epilogue	106

PART 2
THIRTY-MINUTE FRIENDS
People I Meet Again Along the Pathways of My Mind

Prologue	110
A Confession	113
The Aboriginal Man	117
Out of Africa	119
What If They're Lying?	123
Hugs and Kisses All Around	125
From the Children of America to the Children of India	128
He'd Want to Be Buried in His Uniform	133
Look up: What Do You See?	136
Roses Are Red . . .	138
Rosetta Stone	142
Joe from Petaluma and Grandpa the Goat Farmer	144
The Whole World Would Be Pretty	148
Now That's Gifted	150
God Has Left the Room	153
Preach It Brother	156
Adventure to Auckland	160
Honorary Māori	163
It Is a Goat Leg	166
An Indonesian Chanukah	169
Why Are You Laughing	172
What is it Like to Live in a Muslim Country?	174
A New Call to Service	177
You Are Weisser	179
Sometimes There is No Good Answer	183
I'm Teaching Him Because. . .	185
They'll Never Know	188
New York Deli Comes to the Prairie	192
The Seed Corn of Life	198
Off to Oaxaca	203
Fishing with Eduardo	206
Loco and My Meditation Partners	208

My Big Family Goes to Museo de Tortuga	210
Leaving Paradise	212
George Washington Carver James	214
I'm from Nebraska	219
Ritchie Lyman and the Quest for Equality	224
The Quintessential Jewish Festival	228
HUAC Comes to Town	232
Keeping Kosher	235
Honorary Italian	238
Thirty-Minute Friends - Epilogue	242
About the Author—Rabbi Michael Weisser	247

For my dad, Rabbi Michael Weisser, zichrono livracha—
May his memory be for a blessing.
Your voice lives on in these pages,
your spirit in every story.
You taught us that love is stronger than hate,
and that even the smallest moments hold divine meaning.

To our family—thank you for your steadfast love,
for holding each other through sorrow and joy
as we brought this book into the world.

And for Mr. Levine,
whose humble wisdom and daily grace
quietly shaped our father's path.

—Deborah Weisser
Publisher, Sentient Publications

Prologue

A young man who ran a meditation class once told me: "Yesterday is gone; it cannot be reclaimed. Tomorrow has not yet occurred; it therefore does not exist. So, what have you left?"

On the pages of a calendar, yesterday may be gone, the page removed and thrown away. But the things that happened on the paper day that has been discarded don't end up in the wastebasket with the calendar page. They are stored away, biding their time, waiting to emerge when conditions or thoughts beckon them from their secret places. Yesterday is not gone, so it doesn't need to be reclaimed. Every moment of every yesterday lives in an unexplainable way among the neurons and synapses. Yesterday is always present, in the present. Something happens in whichever moment we may find ourselves and suddenly, amazingly, visions of things from times ago become part of the present moment. That happens, seemingly in random fashion, often unexpected and seldom planned. When it does, yesterday is no longer yesterday. Yesterday is never yesterday; it is part and parcel of today. There is no escaping that, and no need to try.

Tomorrow has not yet occurred because tomorrow cannot occur. There is no such thing as tomorrow, because once we think tomorrow has arrived, tomorrow becomes today. There is no way to experience tomorrow. We can speculate, make plans, march forward, visualize what tomorrow will bring, but tomorrow itself doesn't exist. It's an artificial construct we've created that allows us to think there is something different than today. What we have left after all of that is today, the *now* that is always *now*. A second ago is gone.

Mr. Levine and Me

Tomorrow is a fiction. All there really is, is now. But can we even be sure of this?

Because we have, built into the structure of being human, the capacity and sometimes the ability to jiggle loose memories of moments from what we call our "yesterdays," we can live in all times at once. Memories, like unedited movies, are always flitting about somewhere near moments of consciousness. If we stub a toe against a table leg, a movie of some other toe stubbing, or some other painful moment, plays for us. This happens a lot, and mostly we don't think much about it. The movie stops almost as soon as it begins, and we go about doing what we are doing, perhaps with a throbbing toe for a while.

Other scenes from these mental movies play for more than just a moment. This is when the unreclaimable past emerges in the mysterious realm of memory, surfaces, and remains a while. At such times we are living both yesterday and today in simultaneous harmony. Memories at such moments are not from some time long ago, but feel as if (and are) the reality of one place in a life merging with the reality of another place in that same life. I can't prove this to anyone. I don't need to prove it to myself.

The pages that follow and the words that are on them refer, mostly, to a time seventy or so years ago. More than 25,000 calendar pages have been discarded since then. The multitudes of experiences from then did not go into the wastebasket with them. Mr. Levine, the words he spoke to a young boy, and the many other experiences you'll encounter in the pages ahead are real for me right now, not just in some dimly lighted past. My memories of him and some of his words, even though from such a long time ago, are part of the moment that is, for me, today.

Growing up on the Avenue

I grew up in New Haven, Connecticut, around Legion Avenue. It was once a vibrant working-class neighborhood that was ethnically not very diverse. The people there were mostly Italian or Jewish, with a sprinkling of others: a handful of Black families, a few Puerto Ricans, and one Chinese family that I can remember. Everyone got along and there was rarely any trouble around there.

We were all pretty much in the same boat. I'm talking about the early 1950s. There were no computers, no cell phones, or iPads. They hadn't even been thought of yet. There weren't many television sets either, certainly none that showed programs in color. Many of the families around there didn't own cars. Vacations meant time to hang around the neighborhood, or maybe, if it was summertime, a trolley ride to the beaches on Long Island Sound or Savin Rock, the little amusement park that was nearby at the end of the trolley line.

The homes on the side streets off Legion Avenue were mostly wood frame covered with clapboards and painted various colors. Many of them were two- or three-family homes, with the owner living on the first floor and others renting the second- or third-floor apartments. Three generations of the same family lived in some of the houses, with grandparents on the first floors, and sons and daughters and their families upstairs. This was especially true of some of the Italian families. It probably made Sunday dinners a little easier to manage.

I think it's our great loss as a society that city neighborhoods like that don't exist anymore. Driving to shop at the mall or some giant supermarket or going to McDonald's or Olive Garden for a bite to eat is just not the same, especially now when no one talks to each other and people think that "friending" someone electronically equals a relationship. Places like Legion Avenue were real.

I knew every inch of the avenue, at least the part of it that was my stomping ground, which was only about five or six blocks long. My grandparents lived just around the corner from one end of it, in the first-floor apartment of a two-story brownstone row house. My uncle Henry and aunt Ann lived upstairs with my cousin Louise. I used to pitch pennies against the stoop with some of my friends there sometimes. For a while, my mother and stepfather, and my brother and I, lived in a small apartment building just around the corner from there. My sister was finishing up high school and living in Guilford, about twenty miles away, at the home of a friend. The rest of us had come back to New Haven after living on a chicken farm run by my grandparents' friends, Katherine and Nicolai Lubenetz. We called him Uncle Nick and we called her Chuhchuh. Why we had been living in Guilford on a chicken farm is another story for another time.

We lived on the third floor of our building. I remember that because carrying groceries or laundry up the stairs, or the trash down to the alley, were chores that often fell to me. The apartment was small, but there was a living room, three bedrooms, and a kitchen with a linoleum floor that was big enough for a table and chairs. The table was covered with what they used to call oilcloth. It felt a little crowded when everyone was home at the same time, but it was an okay place to live.

It wasn't crowded most of the time, though. My stepfather Morris left the house early each morning to catch the bus downtown, where he worked at a shoe store. My mother left soon after to catch a different bus that would get her over to Whalley Avenue, where she worked as the cashier at a luncheonette. My brother and I came back to an empty apartment when we finished up with our paper routes each morning and made some breakfast before heading off to school. It would have been crowded on the weekends except for the fact that my brother and I were out of the house most of the day. Looking back, I think it was a pretty good life.

There aren't any neighborhoods like Legion Avenue anymore. It was a few blocks of shops, surrounded by residential streets. There were a couple of Catholic churches nearby, and on the avenue itself a small Jewish Community Center that had once been the New Haven Teacher's College. My sister studied there for a semester when she rejoined us after high school until the teacher's college closed and became part of the state university system at a different location near Beaver Pond Park on the other side of town. That's when it became the Jewish Community Center, which remained until a new center was built on Chapel Street near the Yale campus, complete with a swimming pool, duckpin alleys, basketball and handball courts, and lots of activities for all ages.

I'm not sure why most of the kids I thought of as friends were Italian. Maybe it was because I thought they were more sure of themselves than the Jewish kids I knew. Maybe I was a little jealous of their confidence and wanted to be more like them. Maybe it was connected to the fact that Uncle Nick, my grandfather's best friend, once cautioned me and my brother not to tell anyone we were Jewish. That was when we lived on his farm, but I still remembered it.

It's a little strange to me that I recall so much about that place, especially since I spent just a few childhood years around there, and also because it doesn't exist anymore. It was probably no more than ten years after my family moved away from Legion Avenue that most of it was torn down for a highway expansion that didn't actually happen for decades. That was in the era of 1960s urban renewal that didn't really renew anything, just tore things down. It's sad to think that that once-bustling place was bulldozed before the plan for the highway expansion was scrapped or any plans for the neighborhood's improvement were implemented. All the stores I remember, and most of the houses, were destroyed in the name of progress. The neighborhood of my childhood that comes to me in flashes of memory became a wasteland, its shops gone, its people displaced.

Mr. Levine and Me

But even with all that, I still think about the place sometimes. Maybe it's part of getting old. Maybe I think of Legion Avenue in a subconscious need to put myself back into the almost mythical good old days that I probably remember as better than they actually were. Or perhaps the good old days really were the good old days. When I think about the old neighborhood with its couple of blocks of shops surrounded by side streets with their two- and three-family houses, floods of images, some wonderful and some not so much, come into focus.

I can see the faces of some of the neighborhood fixtures. The hefty blond-haired matron with bright-red lipstick and a ready smile, who was always behind the counter at M&T Appetizing, was one of them. The name of that store came from the initials of the people who owned it: Meyer and Thelma. I saw Thelma almost every Sunday morning when my stepfather Morris and I stopped there to get smoked fish like lox along with cheeses cut from huge blocks of goodness, and pickled herring with onions in wine sauce.

Thinking about Thelma now somehow, inexplicably, releases memories of the nameless Italian men who hung out at the luncheonette, drinking coffee and smoking cigars and looking like, to me at least, a gathering of the Mob. They probably weren't gangsters, except maybe one or two of them. For instance, the guy who was called Midgie Renault, whose claim to fame was that he had once been a federal prisoner who escaped being convicted of anything.

I remember Mr. Kaplan, who owned the fruit market on the corner; Mrs. Goldberg, who had the produce store; Barney Breyer, the butcher; Max Wax, the grocer; my friends Bobby and Joey, and our buddy who we called Ash Wednesday because of the prominent mole in the middle of his forehead. All of them on the avenue. All of them familiar then and now, so many years later.

Once Morris and I got a few things for our Sunday morning ritual in our shopping bag we stopped at the newsstand down the street to pick up the Sunday papers: the *New Haven Register*, the *New York Times,* and the *Herald Tribune,* and sometimes the Sunday edition

Growing up on the Avenue

of the *Daily News*. It was an almost religious thing at my house for everyone to read newspapers. My mother always had first dibs on the crossword puzzles. She almost always completed the Sunday Times puzzle, and she did it with a pen! The last stops as we headed home each Sunday morning were two of the bakeries. We'd get big flaky danish pastries filled with blueberries or peaches or cherries or cheese from one of them, Tikotski's, and bagels, plain of course, at the other, the one where Mr. Levine was.

On the way home for our Sunday ritual of noshing and reading, we passed by a couple of the other fixtures. Mr. Kaplan's fruit market, where a kid could always get a free apple. Mrs. Goldstein's produce store with its barrels of kosher dill pickles and pickled green tomatoes (a kid could get a free pickle there just by dipping a hand in one of the barrels). We passed by Barney Breyer's butcher shop, where my grandmother always told Mr. Breyer to keep his thumb off the scale. And of course, Max Wax & Sons Grocery, home of the best midget salamis in the world, made in the store and famous, along Legion Avenue anyway. Those were the days!

Mr. Levine

Most of all, from way back when I was a kid growing up on the avenue, I remember Mr. Levine. More importantly I think, I remember some of the things he said to me when I was a very young kid of ten, eleven, not more than twelve years old, sweeping out the bakery after school each day to earn a quarter. That along with my paper route and any other odd job I could find somehow made me feel like the richest kid in the neighborhood. I wasn't, but I liked to think I was. A quarter a day meant something then.

I've thought about Mr. Levine once in a while throughout my life. I only knew him for a small part of my life, but I've also known him for the rest of my life because he told me all sorts of things that helped me to understand what was going on in the moment. I'm sure he didn't know his words would stay with me forever, even though he prefaced his advice, almost every time, with these words, intoned with his heavy Yiddish accent: *"Michael, I'm gonna tell you something, and I want you should remember it for the rest of your life."* I can hear that gravelly voice and Yiddish accent every time Mr. Levine comes to mind, and I remember how he pronounced "want" as if it were spelled "vaunt."

It's almost as if he's somehow with me when he, or something he said seventy years ago, comes to mind, even though I know he is long dead. I guess, in some unknown way, everyone who comes up as a memory is alive again, at least for the moments when the memory is present. I think that's one reason Jewish religious practice includes observing the anniversary of a loved one's death by lighting a memorial candle and saying a special prayer. When you do that,

Mr. Levine

the person you memorialize is somehow once again with you. Every time you pass the memorial candle flickering in its little glass, the person comes back to life in your mind. Memory is a strange and beautiful thing, and also pretty mysterious.

Seven decades have passed since I first heard Mr. Levine's words of advice or admonition as a kid sweeping the floor of the bakery. Sometimes, when I'm trying to figure something out, his words magically arise to try and show me the way. Over the years, I've repeated some of his advice to others when they were faced with some problem or other. Their plight seemed to open a mysterious channel to Mr. Levine, and some bit of wisdom he'd passed along to me when I was a child would come flowing out from me to someone who needed to hear it. Often I didn't realize they were his words until after I said them, and at such times he was as real to me as if he were standing there beside me. As I've said, it's been seventy years since the last time Mr. Levine guided me through something or another, but I think his words likely had some important impact upon those who heard them second-hand from me.

So, who was Mr. Levine?

He was a man who ran one of the bakeries on Legion Avenue. He was always there. When I got to know him he already seemed old to me, but at my age then, anyone whose hair had turned gray seemed old. He was definitely gray haired and gruff and kindly at the same time. Any kids who came into the bakery with their parents were always rewarded with a free cookie, just for being a kid, if Mr. Levine was behind the counter. I never knew him outside of the bakery. I'm pretty sure, though, that he was the same outside the place as he was inside. I never met anyone from his family, not his wife or his children. Actually, I never knew if he had a wife or children until most of the time I was around him was over. Maybe his customers were like family to him, and some of the neighborhood kids somehow took the place of the children he didn't have. I didn't know for sure then. It could have been, but also, maybe not.

Mr. Levine and Me

Thinking back, I remember him as a simple, good man. I don't think he was educated in the way we usually think of someone being educated. He may have gotten through the eighth grade, as many people did in those days. Very few of the people around Legion Avenue had gone to college. My sister was the first in the history of my family to graduate from college. It was an amazing moment in the life of a family just one generation out from immigration.

Mr. Levine was a Ukrainian Jewish immigrant like my grandparents, who arrived at Ellis Island in the early 1890s. Mr. Levine had made it to America just before the Holocaust. I never knew anything about that for most of the time I knew him because Mr. Levine never spoke of such things to me, except once. He spoke of bread and rolls as if the products that came out of his ovens were who he was. His baked goods were bought by everyone in the neighborhood. Everyone shopped at his bakery, Jews, Italians, and everyone else. It was plain to see that everyone liked him and that he liked them. His quiet ways were matched by the dignity of his being. It oozed out of him and was clear to everyone who knew him.

Even though I never thought about it at the time, my family was poor. We struggled to get by. We moved a number of times because we couldn't pay the rent. I didn't realize a lot of that back then but learned it later in life. It's just the way it was. Because of our situation my brother and I were always looking for ways to earn a little money. There was usually no money at home for movies or milk shakes, and no one thought to whine about that fact. It was the same with a lot of my friends. We were all in pretty much the same situation. For a while I had two paper routes, one in the morning and another in the afternoon. In the summer I went around with an old, borrowed rotary push mower and cut grass for a few people. Once in a while I got lucky enough to pump gas at a nearby Esso station. Whatever I was able to earn in those ways was mine to spend however I wanted. When I had to give up my afternoon paper route because the route manager gave it to another kid, I was lucky enough to walk into the bakery and ask Mr. Levine if he needed any help.

Mr. Levine

I remember how excited I was when he told me I could come and sweep the floor every day after school and on Sunday afternoons, and that he'd give me a quarter each time I did it. That would give me a dollar and a half a week. I felt like I was going to be a young tycoon in the neighborhood.

I think the kindness of that old baker, who let me come and sweep the floor, helped me to learn the value of work. But what I learned about living from Mr. Levine was far more important than what I learned from pushing a broom.

As I mentioned earlier, Mr. Levine always preceded his advice with a reminder that I should remember it for the rest of my life. And I have. Some of his words, spoken to me in his raspy Yiddish accent, still resonate with me even now. I'm an old man myself now, and Mr. Levine is long gone, but he appears in my mind every now and then to help me figure something out. Now there, I think, is a legacy.

Never Take the Rap for the Other Guy

For some reason I enjoyed sweeping up the bakery after school and on Sunday afternoons. It was quiet and peaceful in the empty bakery when I got there. Mr. Levine and one of the ladies who worked there were out in the store taking care of customers, but the bakery itself was empty. No one was there. The bakers, who started their work days at four or five a.m., were finished with their work by the time I got there, so I, broom in hand, had the place to myself. It was like having a private little domain of my own.

I tried to do a perfect job, partly because that's the way I am about most things, and partly because I felt obligated to do so. Mr. Levine trusted me to be the official sweeper, and for a quarter a day, I was intent on not letting him down. He had become an important person in my young life, somehow more like a parental figure than just some old guy who ran a bakery. Once in a while I wondered if he noticed that I swept between the ovens or under the work benches, or that I never left even a little bit of flour anywhere. I never told him how careful I was to do a good job. I just did a good job. He must have been satisfied because I never heard a complaint. He never told me to go back and do it better.

I still remember one of the bakers. His name was Joe Yussel, which I always thought was a pretty strange name. "Yussel" is the Yiddish nickname for Joe or Joseph, so his name was something like "Joe Joe." Joe Yussel was taller than most of the Jewish men

Never Take the Rap for the Other Guy

I saw around the neighborhood, maybe five-eleven or so. He had bushy hair the color of the flour he worked with all day. He was always grumpy and always smelled of whiskey. I know he carried a pint of booze in his back pocket, and he took a nip from it every so often. But it didn't seem to affect his work. Joe was a good baker who knew what he was doing.

When I got to the bakery one day after school, I was surprised to see Joe Yussel still at work at one of the butcher block tables. I didn't know why he was still there working so late in the day, but I didn't ask. Kids know instinctively who they can ask about things, and somehow it was clear to me that Joe Yussel was not a person I should ask about anything.

As I went around the bakery sweeping flour into little piles, I stayed away from where Joe Yussel was working. When I was just about finished with my sweeping, I went around and brushed the piles of flour into a dustpan, dumped them into the trash, and waited for a while, hoping Joe Yussel would finish up soon so I could get my last bit of sweeping done around where he was working. I waited for ten or fifteen minutes and watched him from a distance as he continued cutting chunks of dough with his scraper, rolling them into snaky tubes, and knotting them into rolls.

Finally, I decided I didn't want to keep waiting, so I began to sweep around him as he worked. I must have gotten distracted for a moment, and my broom accidentally bumped into his foot as I swept under the worktable. Joe Yussel spun around and swatted at me with his big flour-covered hand. I ducked and he missed, but then he let loose with a string of profanities as he gave me a pretty hard shove. I got away from him unscathed but seething with anger. I hated him in that moment.

I moved to the other end of the bakery and continued sweeping, even though I'd already swept everywhere except where Joe Yussel was working. I banged my broom on the proof box and against the walls and the big mixer. Then I looked up and there was Mr. Levine, standing near the door that led out from the bakery to the store. I looked at him and he looked at me, and then he gestured that I should come over to him. I leaned my broom against the wall and slowly approached him. I thought I was in trouble because I had been banging the broom around. When I reached him, he opened the door and told me to go into the store with him. I followed, feeling sure he was going to tell me that he didn't need me around anymore, that he would find someone else to sweep the bakery. My first thought was that I was going to lose my dollar and a half a week. But that's not what happened.

Mr. Levine looked at me for a minute. I couldn't tell what he was thinking. When he finally spoke after what seemed to be a long silence that had probably, in reality, been just a few seconds, he asked me, "What's going on? What are you so mad about?"

I think I was near tears, but I told him what Joe Yussel had done and how I wished I could do something to him. I told him I was mad about it. He had tried to hit me, and he had shoved me and cursed me out just because my stupid broom had barely touched his shoe. It wasn't fair. It wasn't right.

Mr. Levine thought about what I had said to him. "So, who are you punishing by being so mad?" he asked. "Yussel pushed you. He swore at you. He yelled at you. And he's still making rolls for a party he's going to have at his house tomorrow." He paused to let that sink in, then went on. "And you, you're running around mad using all that energy thinking you're going to get even. You're not going to get even. Nothing you can do will ever change anything about Joe Yussel. You're beating yourself up for what he did." I thought about what Mr. Levine was telling me. I knew he was right. But I was still mad.

Then Mr. Levine continued.

He began as he always did when he was about to give me some advice. "Michael," he said, "I'm gonna tell you something and I want you should remember it for the rest of your life. Never take the rap for the other guy." He opened the door and I went through it back into the bakery. The door closed behind me, and that was that.

Never Take the Rap for the Other Guy

Joe Yussel was gone. His rolls were rising in the proof box. They would have to go into the oven in about half an hour. I didn't know where he had gone, but I was glad he was not there. I finished sweeping around where Joe Yussel had been working. I wanted to finish up and get out of there before he came back from wherever he had gone. When I finished, I put my broom back in its place, walked out through the store and waved goodbye to Mr. Levine and the lady behind the counter, and began the walk home. It was about four-thirty by then and there weren't many people on the avenue.

As I walked I realized Mr. Levine was right. He was always right. It didn't matter to Joe Yussel that I was mad. He probably wasn't even aware of how angry I was. Even if he was aware, I was sure he didn't care one way or the other. I'd been angry. I'd been banging my broom into things. I was fuming. But Joe Yussel? The object of my anger couldn't care less.

I knew it. My anger, no matter how powerful it felt to me, didn't affect him at all. But it did affect me. It was me who was reliving those moments, not him. It was me who had been huffing and puffing, thrashing, getting red in the face, not him. I was bearing the brunt of the whole thing, punishing myself for what Joe Yussel had done. I was taking the rap for the other guy.

Looking back over my life I recognize that I've experienced anger more than a few times. Sometimes it may have felt good to lash out at someone or something or some event. But the feeling of satisfaction that anger may momentarily bring about is always short lived and never matters even a little bit while it's happening. It's easy to rage and storm, but hard to resolve anything that way. Solutions to problems come through rational thought, not with tirades.

There are some things about anger that have come to me over my lifetime. One thing I've learned is that no one listens to an angry person. You can rant and rave all you want. The effect on others may be fear and loathing, but never respect or consideration.

Think about how we describe ourselves when we're angry. "I got mad," we say once the storm has passed. But what does that mean?

Mr. Levine and Me

Isn't "mad" a synonym for "insane?" When we get mad it's like we've lost our minds for a time. On the other hand, concerns stated rationally (there's that word again) can, at least sometimes, get a fair hearing, maybe even agreement.

Here's something else about being mad: *The thing we are mad about has already happened.* No amount of anger, or anything else, can change that. If we yell and carry on, the thing we are yelling about is still there, already in existence, incapable of disappearing or even fading away. We can solve our problems, for sure, but rarely, if ever, by getting mad. Getting mad prevents us from seeing the path to solutions. It locks whatever we are mad about into place, and unless we take a different approach, it will be forever with us.

I knew two brothers once, members of my congregation in the late 1970s. They both seemed like nice people to me, but at some point they had gotten mad at one another. They stopped speaking to each other. There were no more family dinners, no summer picnics, no visits between their two families. Everyone who knew them learned pretty quickly not to mention one brother to the other, because they knew the result would be an avalanche of grievances. When these two brothers attended a service at the synagogue they sat on opposite sides of the sanctuary, and they didn't speak to one another. Neither of them could live the message of the Day of Atonement, Yom Kippur, and offer forgiveness for whatever it was that drove them to such animosity toward one another. It was a sad thing to see.

These two stubborn brothers were in their seventies when I knew them. I was perhaps thirty-five years their junior. *Still,* I thought, *maybe I can reason with them. Maybe if I just speak with them, they'll come to see the light.* So I called and went to visit the younger of the two.

When I got there, he offered me a cup of coffee and asked me what was up. After we exchanged a few pleasantries (how's the family, the grandchildren, and so on), I said I was concerned about the long-running feud between him and his brother. "Isn't there some way you could forgive him for whatever he did that got you to be so angry with him?"

He answered really abruptly: "I don't want anything to do with him."

I went on and told him I thought it was a mistake and that there must be some way for he and his brother to resolve things. Again he told me he didn't want any part of his brother, and that was it. Finally, I pulled out what I thought were the "big guns," which I thought might convince him.

"You know," I said, "you're both getting up in years. One of you is going to die one of these days. Do you really want to leave it like this?"

He wasn't moved and suggested that I mind my own business.

Later that same day I went to visit with the older of the two brothers. The reception was about the same, although this brother was a little more forthcoming about what was wrong between them. He told me they had been in business together. They had been partners and worked well together for a long time. But when problems befell them and their business, he blamed his brother.

"I got mad at him," he said, "It was all his fault. But did he listen? No. He blamed me for everything. I was mad at him and he got mad at me. There was no way to fix things. So, we went our separate ways, and we're better off for it."

I asked him if he was really sure they were better off. *What had happened to whatever love had existed between them?* They loved each other enough, once, to feel good about being partners, about working together every day for many years. I tried to pull out my big guns on him, too. But as with his brother, it didn't work. They were both committed to the anger, to the animosity, to the blaming.

A couple years later the younger brother suffered a heart attack and died. I had to conduct his funeral service. His brother was there, seated with his wife and children and grandchildren. Beside him were the wife and children and grandchildren of his brother, all of them united in their grief. The older brother was crying. He cried all during the eulogy. He cried at the cemetery as the coffin was lowered into the ground. He cried as he gently, almost lovingly, placed a spadeful of earth on the coffin. Following the burial service everyone gathered at the house his brother had called home. We conducted the brief ritual that is traditional for such gatherings, and afterward, as everyone was getting a cup of coffee or something to eat, he approached me and asked me to step outside so he could tell me something. We went outside and he embraced me with a long, sad hug. "Rabbi," he sobbed, "I will regret for the rest of my life that I didn't make things right with my brother. I should have listened to you. And now it's too late."

I remembered Mr. Levine's words to me when I was mad at Joe Yussel: *Never take the rap for the other guy.* I wished I had spoken those words to these two brothers when both of them were alive, that I had somehow gotten them to understand that each of them was taking the rap for the other, and that they each were punishing themselves for what they thought the other had done. I think that was the essence of what Mr. Levine meant when he told me not to take the rap for the other guy.

You Are Who You Are

I remember who I was back then, and I also remember that I always wanted to be someone else. After all, why would anyone want to be me? Everyone was better than me. I was negative about myself, my abilities, my intelligence, my strength, my talents. I was small. I was scared of things. Those are the images that came up if I thought about myself. I wanted to be big. I wanted to be strong and courageous. But I was none of those things. They were what other people were.

My family and I lived in a succession of apartments. For some reason we moved about once a year. We did that a lot of times. I sometimes wondered if it was somehow my fault that we were always moving. I wanted to live in a permanent place like all my friends did. But that never happened. I got tired of wearing secondhand clothes passed down from a cousin or from my brother. I wanted to wear clothes that nobody had ever worn. If I looked in the mirror, something I usually avoided doing, I saw a skinny kid with thin hair, thin lips, a droopy eye, and a face that, as people used to say, only a mother could love. I really wanted to be someone else. I knew I couldn't be someone else, but it was good regardless to think that maybe I could.

I complained about such things to whoever was willing to listen to the whining of a skinny kid. They'd listen for a minute and then cut me off by telling me they had to go. It didn't stop me from trying, until one day I tried my litany of complaints and self-deprecation out on Mr. Levine. He listened, maybe a little longer than anyone else, until he too cut me off mid-sentence with a wave of his hand.

"What are you moaning about? Do you see me moaning like you? Look at me, what do you see? No, really look. I'm short, I'm almost bald, I got a big schnozzola. I've always known I would never be a good looker. I've been coming to work my whole life at four in the morning. Don't you think I ever wanted to be like other people? Work in an office? Be a nine to fiver? But no, I became a baker. I've been a baker and I'll always be a baker. I make rolls and bagels and bread. I've been lugging sacks of flour around my whole life. My back is always sore. Do you hear me complaining?"

There was a deep silence between us. I had never known Mr. Levine thought those things about himself. He was just Mr. Levine to me. He was the man who let me sweep the bakery. He was the one who gave me a quarter every day. He was the best, and it was hard for me to know that maybe he sometimes felt the same way about himself as I did about myself.

But then he continued. "Everyone is a little bit jealous of somebody. That's just the way it is. The other guy has something you want. He looks the way you want to look. He lives in a nicer place than you do. He's more popular. All that gets you thinking, '*I wish I could be….I wish I could be…..*,' but wishing means nothing. I'm gonna tell you something and I want you should remember it for the rest of your life. You are who you are. You have what you have. And that's it. The other guy is the other guy. He is who he is and he has what he has. And that has nothing to do with you."

Those words burned into my brain that day. *I am who I am*. Even if I want to, I can't change that. Just because I don't like something about myself at a given moment doesn't mean I'm not a valuable part of the world. Even in whatever negative situation I may find myself, I am who I am, and I have what I have. That's a truth, an obvious truth. Thinking about who the other guy is and what the other guy has doesn't change who I am or what I have.

You Are Who You Are

Thinking back on all I heard that day, I learned a couple important lessons. One is to be okay living in my own skin. *I am who I am.* Another is to be satisfied with what I have, even as I may be striving to have other things. *I have what I have.* A third thing I learned that day so long ago seems obvious now, even though it didn't seem so at times during my life. Other people are who they are, and they have what they have, and that, really, has nothing to do with me.

Those few words from Mr. Levine have been a real gift. I don't have to be anyone but myself. I'm okay as I am. I'm not one of the "beautiful people," but I am who I am. I'll never be what they used to call a "matinee idol," but I am who I am. I'm not a muscular athlete, but I am who I am. I could easily come up with a long list of what I'm not, but such a list would have no real meaning. The wonderful attributes of others are something to be admired, of course—for them. My own attributes are also something to be admired, for me.

The same is true about possessions. I drive a car that is now fifteen years old. It's in great shape because I've always been sure to take care of its maintenance. It runs well, and it still looks pretty good. The interior is almost like new and there is not a trace of rust on the car, but still, it's fifteen years old. The clothes I most like to wear have been with me for a lot of years. Some of my favorite sweaters are probably twenty years old, and my favorite jeans and shirts are old enough to be soft and comfortable, even with their worn spots. I live in a comfortable but modest house with furniture that in some cases is older than me. It's good that I'm used to all those things. I have what I have, and that's it. There are people I know with newer cars, beautiful wardrobes that are right in style, homes that are bigger and fancier than mine and filled with expensive furniture. There was a time in my life when I'm sure I would have been envious, but now I'm happy for them. They are who they are and they have what they have. What's that got to do with me?

You Know What You Get from Wanting?

Sometimes we all moan and groan about not having something other people have. We all do it because we are so tied to things. Somehow we've learned to value ourselves by the value of the things we have or by the things we don't have. I don't know exactly why we do it, but I do know that we all do it, at least sometimes. Is it because we are envious? Maybe we do it because we are greedy. Is it out of desire or avarice or something simpler, like wanting for the sake of wanting? I don't really know the answer. I just know that everyone I know, everyone I've ever known, has done it sometimes.

One Christmas my friend Joey's grandparents got him a brand-new bicycle. It was beautiful, with skinny wheels, brake levers on the handlebars, and a three-speed gear shift. It had lights front and back, and one of those skinny, uncomfortable-looking seats. The handlebars were formed in such a way that you had to lean forward to ride. It was special. No one in the neighborhood had a bike like that. Most of my friends and I had junky bikes. Mine was rideable, but it was made up of parts salvaged from old broken bikes people had discarded. I went all over the place on that shabby old bike, and yes, it did get me where I wanted to go. I was glad for Joey, but at the same time I was really jealous of him. I wanted something better. I wanted a bicycle like Joey's.

There was no use talking about a new bike at home. I knew that was not a solution. I heard my parents talking sometimes about how

You Know What You Get from Wanting?

they couldn't pay this bill or that, about how tough things were. My brother and I had learned well that asking for stuff, especially something expensive like a new bicycle, was out of the question. I couldn't whine about it at home, so after a while I did what I thought at the time was the next best thing. I talked about Joey's new bike with Mr. Levine. If anyone would understand, it would be him.

I talked with him about it one afternoon after I finished my sweeping. I complained, I whined, I wished I could have what Joey had. I wanted a bike like his, new and shiny, with all the bells and whistles, with a lot of class. Joey had a new bicycle. I wanted one just like it. I hadn't yet incorporated the lesson of *I am who I am and I have what I have* into my thinking.

Mr. Levine listened to my griping for quite a while, maybe ten or fifteen minutes, until, as always happened, he got tired of hearing the same old song over and over again. He put up his big, gnarled hand, and out came the familiar words: "Michael, I'm gonna tell you something and I want you should remember it for the rest of your life."

I think I held my breath thinking that somehow Mr. Levine was going to tell me some magical way to get a bicycle like Joey's. Instead he said, "You know what you get from wanting? You get old." Then he turned, went back behind the counter, waved at me, and said, "See you tomorrow."

This bit of advice, or whatever it was, didn't make any sense to my eleven-year-old brain in the moment I heard it. *What does getting old have to do with wanting? Or, what does wanting have to do with getting old?* It took me quite a long time to make sense of it, but eventually I understood. Wanting is just wanting. Nothing comes from wanting on its own. Wanting is static. It accomplishes nothing, unless we think of wanting itself as a desirable thing. Wanting, without action, brings nothing your way. It's a useless exercise.

The only cure for wanting is not wanting. You have to forget about whatever it is you find yourself wanting, or to somehow acquire the thing that you're wanting. In my case, it meant either

Mr. Levine and Me

forgetting about Joey's new bicycle or getting one for myself somehow. Since getting one for myself was not really possible, and I knew it, I tried my best to stop being envious of Joey's good fortune.

But I ultimately did get a bicycle that was even better than Joey's. Strangely enough, Mr. Levine had something to do with that. He didn't get a bike for me, but he helped me to do what I needed to do when the opportunity arose.

Right around the time Joey got his new bicycle for Christmas and set off my spasm of envy, I joined the Boy Scouts. I was not yet twelve, the age at which you could become a Boy Scout, but they let me join anyway. The troop met in the basement of the synagogue my family attended, but it was not a Jewish troop. Boys of all backgrounds were part of it. After I'd been there for about a month attending the weekly meeting to learn about knot tying and how to make a campfire or pitch a pup tent, the Scoutmaster made a big announcement. There was going to be a Jamboree where all the scouts could demonstrate the skills they had learned. The public, at least those who bought a ticket, would be there and at the end of the day there would be a pizza party for the boys. It sounded fun, and all of us in the troop were pretty excited.

Then the scoutmaster said something that caught my interest. Each boy was going to be responsible for selling tickets to the Jamboree to family and friends, and the scouts who sold the most tickets would win a prize. The third-place prize was a pocket knife. The second-place prize was a portable radio. The first-place prize was a Raleigh English bicycle. When I heard that I started breathing hard. I was going to win that bicycle!

At the end of the meeting that evening each boy was asked how many tickets they wanted. Some kids said ten, a few said twenty or twenty-five, and one kid said fifty. When it came time for me to speak up, I blurted out, "Two hundred."

Everyone laughed.

No one could possibly sell two hundred tickets. They were fifty cents apiece. The more people laughed and razzed me, the more

You Know What You Get from Wanting?

I was determined to take two hundred tickets. So the scoutmaster counted out tickets for everyone and gave two hundred to me. He said good luck, and we ended the meeting.

Over the next few days, I sold some tickets. My grandparents bought two. My uncle Harry bought one, but Aunt Millie made him buy another. The same happened with Uncle Henry and Aunt Ann. Morris, my stepfather, bought a ticket, and I was even able to get my sister to buy one. I was happy that I had sold eight tickets so quickly, but then I realized I was fresh out of relatives. I was able to sell a few more to a couple of my mother's friends. My grand total had grown to eleven, and I didn't know who else I could approach. I resigned myself to my fate. I'd probably come in last, but worse, the other kids would laugh at the "big shot" who thought he was going to sell two hundred Jamboree tickets.

The next time I went to sweep the bakery I told Mr. Levine about my failure as a salesman. He listened and then chuckled a little bit.

"Michael," he said, "I think you're going about it the wrong way." When I asked him what I could do, he gave me a plan. "Don't sweep the bakery tomorrow. Take the bus downtown and go into Shartenberg's, you know, the furniture store on the corner of State Street. Ask to see the manager. Tell him how good it would be if the store supported the Boy Scouts and then ask him to buy ten tickets. Tell him that the stores that support the scouts will be honored at the Jamboree. See what happens."

I asked him if he really thought that would work and he smiled.

"Of course it will work. And after it does, go to every store downtown that you can and do the same thing. Make sure you talk to the manager, not some clerk. You'll sell a lot of tickets." I thanked him and said I'd do it. Then he told me to take two days off from sweeping if I needed to, and added, "Don't forget to wear your Boy Scout uniform."

It worked like a charm. The manager at Shartenberg's bought ten tickets. So did the folks at the department store and A.S. Beck Shoes, and Frenchie's shoes, and a couple of jewelry stores, and

Mr. Levine and Me

every other place I could get to during those two afternoons, even the Loew's Poli Theater. When I was done I realized I had sold one hundred and seventy-seven tickets in just two afternoons. That, added to the eleven I'd convinced my family and my mother's friends to buy, made a grand total of one hundred and eighty-eight. It felt like a miracle had happened. Mr. Levine was a genius.

A few weeks later, when it came time for all the boys to turn in their money and leftover unsold tickets, I gave the scoutmaster a lunch bag with ninety-four dollars and twelve unsold tickets in it. The kid who came in second had sold fifty tickets, all of them to his parents, and I think the third-place kid had sold something like thirty-five. The Jamboree took place a few weeks later and at the very end of that day the prizes were awarded. I rode home on my brand-new Raleigh English bicycle, the best bicycle in the neighborhood. As I rode down Legion Avenue I remembered a phrase I had read in some book: "Proud as a peacock." I was proud, and like a peacock, I was strutting as I rode that bike down the avenue.

I think learning that lesson—*You know what you get from wanting? You get old*—at such an early age was very important. Wanting simply uses up time, one of our few precious possessions, and it provides nothing in return. Because of Mr. Levine's advice about salesmanship I'd been able to land on one of the two antidotes to wanting. You remember what they are:

The only cure for wanting is not wanting," and:

"The only ways to stop wanting are to forget about whatever it is you find yourself wanting, or to somehow acquire the thing that you're wanting."

But there is another lesson in all of this. I so clearly remember riding that bike home from the Jamboree, and how proud I was of my new possession. But I also remember that once I had ridden that

You Know What You Get from Wanting?

bike maybe a few dozen times, it magically became just another bike.

Mr. Levine's words, my success with ticket sales, my feeling of pride at having something brand new, and later my feeling of "So what?" after a time led me to some other realizations. One of these was that possession has no real meaning. Nobody really owns anything. We just have the use of things for a while and then, inevitably, those things we think we own but which we are just using for a time pass on to someone else who will get to use them for a while. The desire for possessions is, I've come to believe, a fool's errand. At some point, enough really is enough.

I've wanted for things lots of times in my life. Now that I'm an old man I don't do much wanting anymore, because I know what I get from wanting. I get old. And you know what? I'm already there.

The Truth Will Win

The back of the dormitory for the nursing school of St. Raphael's Hospital faced George Street near the corner of Sherman Avenue. Between it and the street there was an empty grass-covered double lot. It was the perfect place for kids to play touch football, and many of my weekend days were spent there. Bobby, Joey, Ash Wednesday and I, along with a bunch of other kids, would meet up there for a game. We loved playing there because sometimes some of the nursing students would come to their windows overlooking our playing field to watch and cheer us on. When that happened we felt like we were playing at the Yale Bowl. It was great to have an audience to show off for.

One Sunday afternoon, after Bobby, Joey, and Ash Wednesday got out of church, we met up and headed over to George Street. We rode up Legion Avenue to Scranton Street and then to George Street and made our way to the playing field. When we got there some other kids had already arrived. They hadn't started playing yet because none of them had brought a football, but Bobby had his with him. We chose up sides and took to the field of battle. As we played I think all of us kept checking the dorm windows to see if any of the nursing students were watching. When we noticed them, we played harder. I guess we were trying to impress them.

We had played for a couple hours, and the score was tied. If one team scored, the other team followed with a score of its own. At some point one of the kids said it was time to call it a day. It was after five o'clock and he had to go home. But everyone started yelling that we had to finish the game. It was a tough decision for me.

The Truth Will Win

Sweep the bakery or finish the game. Finish the game won the argument. I reasoned that I could sweep the bakery late and it wouldn't matter since there was no one working after three. It would be okay. We all agreed the game would be over the next time someone scored and broke the tie. Finally someone scored. Most of us turned and waved to the couple of nursing students who were still watching from their dorm windows. Then we went to our bikes and headed off to wherever we were going.

I made my way back to Legion Avenue, and when I reached the bakery it was already closed. I knocked on the door a few times just in case someone was still there, but there was no answer. I went home wondering what Mr. Levine must have thought when I didn't show up.

The next day after school I went straight to the bakery, just as I had done each school day for the past five or six months. I went in and began to sweep the floor. After a few minutes, the door to the store opened and Mr. Levine came into the bakery. He slowly walked over to me. He wasn't smiling, but had a hard look that I'd never seen before on his face. He didn't speak as he approached and when he was near enough he reached out, took the broom from my hand, and started sweeping himself. I didn't say anything for a minute as he quietly swept. The only thing I could hear was the sound of the push broom's bristles as they moved across the floor. It was strange. I wondered what I should do, and finally I asked Mr. Levine why he was sweeping.

He stopped sweeping and leaned on his broom. He gave me a long look with that stern expression still on his face. I think I was getting a little scared. Finally Mr. Levine spoke. "Why am I doing this?" he asked. "I did it yesterday too. I was sweeping the bakery before you were born. I know how to do it." And then he asked, "Where were you yesterday? What happened?"

I lied to him. I lied to Mr. Levine, the best adult in my life, the man who had been so kind to me, who trusted me and let me earn a quarter every day. I looked straight at him as I created my cover

Mr. Levine and Me

story. I told him my mother had asked me to sort and fold a big bag of laundry and it took longer than I thought it would, and when I finished I came straight to the bakery but it had already closed. I apologized a few times and waited for Mr. Levine to tell me that it was all right. I thought he would say it was okay and everything would get back to normal. I guess I thought it was a reasonable story and that he would believe it. It sounded good to me. But he said nothing for a little while. All the time I'd been telling him my lie he just kept pushing the broom, kept sweeping the floor. That hard expression never left his face. He had never looked at me like that before.

When he finally stopped sweeping and spoke, I knew I had done the wrong thing by lying to him. "Michael," he said, "You're not telling me the truth, are you?"

I didn't say anything. I just stood there looking down at my feet until he spoke again.

"You know why I know you're not telling me the truth?" he said. "Because when you didn't show up I called your mother to see if you were okay, and she told me she didn't know where you were. So you were doing something else and you decided to lie to me about it. I'm not happy about that."

I looked at Mr. Levine, and I realized that the hard look on his face was not anger. No, it was disappointment. I got up my courage and told him I made up that story because I thought he would be mad at me if I told him the truth, that I was playing football with my friends and put off sweeping until it was too late. I was crying when I told him I was sorry. His face softened, and then he spoke those familiar words: "Michael, I'm gonna tell you something and I want you should remember it for the rest of your life. If you tell the truth, the truth will win. If you tell a lie, the truth will win."

Mr. Levine handed me the broom and walked away. As he disappeared through the door that led to the store, I felt a very strong sense of remorse and shame. I knew I had disappointed this man I looked up to, and I believed I would never be able to regain his trust.

The Truth Will Win

When I was alone in the bakery, just me and my broom, I remembered something my grandfather once told me. He once told me that a liar is always a liar. Even when a liar is not telling a lie, he is still a liar. My grandfather told me that if a person lies all the time, or even just some of the time, no one can trust him, because it's impossible for anyone to know if what's coming out of his mouth is true or not. When someone lies to you again and again, trust is eroded, and it becomes more than difficult to find reasons to trust that person. Once we know a person is a liar we will always ask ourselves, *Is this true?* or *Is this a lie?* every time such a person tells us anything at all.

My grandfather wasn't telling me all that because I had lied to him, but just because he wanted to teach me something important. Thinking about it there in the bakery, I thought my grandfather was like Mr. Levine somehow. I remembered how my grandfather ended that conversation: "Michael," he said, "You can never trust a liar. It would be a good thing if you always remember that."

Mr. Levine never mentioned my lie again. I think he forgave me because he once told me that if you forgive someone you should never mention whatever you forgave them about again. It may be that he forgave me because I was a kid, and kids are sometimes foolish. I didn't forgive myself, though, for a long time.

The lesson I learned that day has come back to me more than once over the years, and I've always been grateful that I knew that *if you tell a lie, the truth will win.*

Brothers and Friends

My brother David and I started life together. He was almost six and I was almost four when our father left our mother for another woman. When that happened, the only way our mother was able to cope with her situation was to place David and me, and our sister Sylvia, in an orphanage, the Jewish Home for Children. Sylvia, seven years older than me, got out of there after a year or so to live with our mother because Sylvia was old enough to pretty much look after herself. David and I were in the orphanage for a couple years longer, until our mother married the man who became our stepfather. That's when we moved to a chicken farm about twenty miles from New Haven. The farm was owned by my grandfather's best friend from the old country (the man I've mentioned earlier, who we called Uncle Nick). David and I were close when we lived on the farm. We had to be, I guess, since there were no other kids around. We became, at least for the few years we lived on the farm, brothers who were also friends.

Our father drove a city bus for the Connecticut Company then, and bus drivers wore military-looking uniforms in those days. In later years when my mother spoke of the other woman, Edith, who my father had eventually married and had several children with, my mother always said that Edith couldn't resist a man in uniform. I didn't get the joke at the time.

David and I hardly ever saw our father when we were growing up. He was just not part of our lives, except once in a while after we had moved back to New Haven. If we happened to get on whatever bus he was driving, he'd let us ride for free. After we were teenagers we never saw him at all. The only time I ever spent more than an hour with him was when I was in my forties and my then wife talked me into looking him up during a visit to New Haven. My father and I met at a place near downtown and had coffee together. We talked a little bit, but it was a pretty strange experience since I didn't really know him. It was like being with an old guy who was a stranger. All he really wanted to do was show me pictures of his other family. I don't think my brother David ever met up with him at all after childhood. We never spoke about it, so I don't know for sure.

One day I talked with Mr. Levine about my brother David. By the time I started my job sweeping the bakery, my brother and I had almost nothing to do with one another. We lived under the same roof with our mother and stepfather, and we liked to visit with our grandparents and with our uncles and cousins once in a while, but that was about it. We had different friends and different interests. As we got older, we did less and less with each other. That's probably the way it is with many brothers. Interests diverge, circles of friends develop, different paths are taken.

My brother has been coming to the fore recently because a couple months ago he breathed his last and went on to his next stage of existence. His farewell took place in England and his wife made sure the funeral service was available for streaming since nobody on this side of the pond was going to make the journey to England for the funeral. I was able to hear the words of praise spoken by his friends and learn some things I'd never known about David. The love of brothers traveled through the mystical aura that surrounds us. The connections between us, that had always been there even if seldom noticed, were as strong as the love of brothers can be.

David was almost two years older than me, and even though we weren't very close, I always looked up to him. He knew how to do things much better than I did. He dressed sharp. He had a ruddy complexion and black hair in tight curls. Actually, he was pretty handsome. He was popular with everyone, especially the girls.

Mr. Levine and Me

I was pretty much his opposite. I was small and skinny. I never thought about what I was wearing, just threw something on and that was good enough. I never thought I was very good looking with my pale skin and thin lips and straight, limp hair, even though my mother and grandmother were always telling me how handsome I was. I knew they were just saying that because that's what moms and grandmothers did.

David was smart and always got good grades. Me? Not so much. I really disliked school, except for when I was in the fifth and sixth grades with Miss Maskel, the best teacher I ever knew. David was talented, too. He taught himself how to play the trumpet, and by the time he was fourteen or so he was immersed in jazz and knew all the great jazz players by name. I never learned to play an instrument, but I once sang in a doo wop group that I and a couple of friends had put together. The name of that group was Two Days and a Night. We gave it that name because it was made up of two White kids and a Black kid, something pretty much unheard of back then.

I spoke with Mr. Levine about my brother sometimes. He always listened as if he understood. I wondered if he had a brother of his own, but he never talked about his own family. One time when I was telling Mr. Levine something about my brother, he reminded me that my brother was my brother and I was who I was (that was a lesson I'd heard before from him in a different context). Then he told me something I didn't understand at the time. He didn't preface it with his admonition that I "should remember it for the rest of my life." He didn't have to. He did that so often that I heard it even if he didn't say it. But he told me that somewhere in the Bible, in the Book of Proverbs, he had once read, "...there is a friend more devoted than a brother."

He told me to think about that because brothers often go their separate ways in life. They're together when they are little children, but even then they compete for attention from Mama or Papa. They are together as they grow up, but at some point they find different things to do. They're busy with their friends. Maybe they find a soul mate, fall in love, get married, have children, and live their lives mostly, and sometimes completely, separate from one another. Even if they are pretty close, as the years go by they may get together on holidays or birthdays. They see each other at bar mitzvahs or weddings or funerals, and in between they may rarely, if ever, see each other. It's not because they don't like each other, it's just that they're busy with what is going on in their separate lives.

I remember thinking about those words from Mr. Levine. I always thought about what he told me. I tried to compare some of my boyhood friends with my brother. I didn't think Bobby or Joey or Ash Wednesday were any better or any worse than my brother David. They were all okay, my friends and my brother, but it was definitely true that I spent more time with them than I did with him. I didn't really understand at the time the point Mr. Levine was making about friends being somehow more devoted than brothers. For a long time afterward I didn't think much about it.

As the years went by, Mr. Levine's words came back to me once in a while. My brother and I joined the Army at almost the same time. He was eighteen and a half and I was seventeen. We had different experiences during our time in the service. I never left the United States. He ended up stationed in Belgium and got to visit different places in Europe. I was granted an early out and he stayed in the service for three years. When David returned to civilian life he established himself as a musician, found a soulmate, lived in Los Angeles for a few years and then moved with his wife to England where he lived for the rest of his life, finding a new soul mate after his divorce, getting gigs at pubs and cruise ships and in hotels in Istanbul and Ankara. He lived the life he wanted to live and, I think, really made a go of it. When I left the Army I lived a life that was filled with several years of troubles until I finally got things sorted out and traveled along a better path, eventually studying at a seminary and following my calling as a cantor and rabbi for many years.

Over the years David and I didn't communicate very much. He was in England and I was in America. I never visited him in his adopted country, but he came "home" twice, once for a random visit back in the late 1980s, and again in 2007, to be with family when our mother died. We were together in New Haven again, with our sister and her children and my children as well. My sister wanted me to conduct the funeral service for our mother, and I did. Not surprisingly, it was difficult. Mothers are the ones we've known the longest, the first person we have any connection to. When the ceremony was over, my brother David, tears in his eyes, embraced me and said, "I didn't know you could sing like that. Mom is proud." I think those were the most important words I ever heard from David, and I cherish them still.

I think that when Mr. Levine quoted from Proverbs and told me "...there is a friend more devoted than a brother," he may have been right, at least partly so. He was correct that a real friend is always ready to help in any circumstance. Friends demonstrate a certain kind of constant loyalty and are supportive of one's choices even if they may disagree with those choices. A good friend is always ready to give advice and remains a good friend even if their advice is rejected. Friends share the wisdom acquired in their lifetimes and are always ready to be good companions, in good times as well as bad times. These qualities are rare, to be sure, and if we ever encounter people who manifest them we should embrace them, cherish them, and try our best to emulate them and strive to become people who also manifest those characteristics.

But here's where I think Mr. Levine may have fallen short this one time. A brother, a good brother, whether near or far, in constant touch or not, can evoke the feelings that only come from whatever magic is inherent in a shared childhood. Maybe it has something to do with the fact of emergence into life from the same womb. I'm not sure of the why, or the how, but I am sure of this truth. The love of one brother far exceeds the love of a hundred friends.

Very Perfect

When I began as the bakery floor sweeper I was at the end of the fifth grade. I continued my sweeping all during the sixth grade and into junior high school. (There was no such thing as middle school then; kids went from elementary school to junior high and then on to high school.) I was lucky during my fifth- and sixth-grade years to be the student of Miss Maskel, the best teacher I can remember out of all the teachers I've experienced. I learned English, Arithmetic, Science, Geography, History, Arts and Music with that teacher. When I think back on the two school years I spent with her, I remember them as a bright spot in a pretty dim world.

Except for those years, I wasn't much interested in school. I was just lucky that at the same time I was going to class, I was also learning important things at the bakery. Mr. Levine is the other best teacher I remember. Miss Maskel got me to want to know things I didn't know before. Mr. Levine got me to know things I needed to know that I didn't know I needed to know.

Miss Maskel taught tolerance. Mr. Levine also. Miss Maskel taught love of the other. Mr. Levine also. Miss Maskel taught good citizenship. Mr. Levine also. Miss Maskel used books and maps and music and art and I remember her as one who opened me up to the idea that every day can be a learning day. Mr. Levine used short sayings, many of which I still remember, and I remember him as one who tried to send me in a good direction. If I had to give them grades, they'd both get A pluses. Miss Maskel had to write my grades on a report card. Mr. Levine graded me with a smile or a frown.

Mr. Levine and Me

When I was in school the grading system was "A, B, C, D, and F." But my grandmother once told me that when Uncle Harry and Uncle Henry went to school it was different. In those days, the grades went "E, VG, G, P, and VP," which stood for "Excellent, Very Good, Good, Poor, and Very Poor." That was the grading system in those days. Everyone laughed when Grandma told the story of Uncle Harry's report card filled with P's and VP's. Grandma and Grandpa didn't know what it meant, and Uncle Harry tried to convince them that that 'P' meant 'Perfect' and 'VP' meant 'Very Perfect.' He didn't get away with it. My mother, their sister, told on him.

One Sunday afternoon in the bakery I finished up my sweeping pretty early. Mr. Levine was in the store, and there were not many customers coming in or out. It was always slow late on Sunday afternoons, and sometimes I'd stick around after my sweeping was done and just talk for a while with Mr. Levine. He was one of the few grownups outside of my family who would listen to me for more than a minute or two, and I guess I needed an ear like his now and then. I always had some question or some problem I wanted to talk about and Mr. Levine usually made time for me. My mother was always either too busy or too tired, and I had long given up asking her about much of anything. I knew she loved me, but I also knew, even when I was very young, that her life had been hard.

I think she suffered right along with me and my brother and sister when we had to stay in the orphanage after my father walked out on us. I knew, as soon as I was old enough to know anything, how hard it was to be a divorced woman in those days. Even though I loved my stepfather and I knew he loved me too, he was not the sort of person I thought was approachable about kid stuff. He was good to me and worked hard to try and provide the family with what we needed, but life was hard for him, too. I probably could have talked with Miss Maskel, but school was out at two thirty each day and she, just like the kids, was ready to go home when the school day came to a close.

Very Perfect

On this day, though, sitting on a stool behind the counter in the store, it was Mr. Levine who wanted to talk. He waved me to one of the tables by the front windows and I sat down there. He came around from behind the counter with a couple of oatmeal raisin cookies and a cup of milk and put them down in front of me. Then he sat down across from me.

"Did you know my name was not always Levine?" he asked. I must have looked surprised, and he quickly added, "It used to be Levytskyi." I looked at him in silence. I wondered why he was telling me this.

"When I was born, my mother named me Dmitro. That's who I was, Dmitro Levytskyi. I'm Ukrainian, like your Bubbe Sofia and your Zayde Mikhail. I came to America around the same time as they did, about fifty years ago. I was Dmitro Levytskyi, Ukrainian. Now I'm David Levine, American. I changed my name right after I was naturalized, after I became a citizen of this country." I knew that lots of immigrants changed their names to seem more American, but still I was surprised to learn that Mr. Levine had done that. He was Mr. Levine, whose first name I hadn't known until that day. How could he be Dmitro Levytskyi?

As I listened to Mr. Levine I remembered the story my mother had once told me about how my grandparents, Bubbe Sofia and Zayde Mikhail, as Dmitro Levytskyi had called them, or Grandma Sophie and Grandpa Michael, as I knew them, had gotten their surnames. She told me that a couple of generations before my grandparents came to this country, when the Russians were in control of Ukraine as they sometimes were, a *ukase*, or edict, came down that everyone in the country had to adopt a surname. Many people were simply named *so and so,* the son or daughter of *so and so*, and had no surname. The people in the cities, like Kyiv, (then commonly known as Kiev), where Grandma Sophie's family was, obeyed and chose surnames that they then registered with the authorities. Her family took the Hebrew word *Livracha* ("for the blessing") and Ukrainianized it to *Lavruk*, and that became their name. My grandfather's family lived in a little village, and the people there ignored the edict until one day some officials, accompanied by a band of Cossacks, showed up and gave everyone in the village a surname that was then registered in the official records. Those officials were apparently not very creative and gave everyone in the village the same name: Ivanov.

When my grandmother arrived in America at the age of thirteen, alone but taken in as a housekeeper for a well-off Ukrainian family in New York, her name was Sofia Lavruk, a name that she kept until she married my grandfather. My grandfather, Mikhail Ivanov, became Michael Ewanuff because that was the way the immigration officer at Ellis Island had spelled it when he arrived at the age of eighteen. My grandfather had left Ukraine, with his parents' blessing, along with his friend Nicolai Lubenetz to avoid being conscripted into the Russian military. He and Nicolai had walked across Europe to France, living on odd jobs until they saved enough to book passage on a tramp steamer to America. My grandmother had been sent alone by her parents to find a better life in America. It's the kind of story that can be repeated millions of times. It's what built the fabric of the United States. Neither of my grandparents ever saw their families again. They wrote letters to them and received answers until the late 1930s, and then they were gone forever, probably victims of the Nazis.

Through his story, I knew Mr. David Levine, or Dmitro Levytskyi, better than ever before. But he was still Mr. Levine to me. Later on, thinking about that Sunday afternoon, the grading systems of Miss Maskel and Uncle Harry came to mind. I gave Dmitro Levytskyi an A, but Mr. Levine got the best of Uncle Harry's grades, VP. Very Perfect!

An Aside

After I had spent about a year and a half of my after-school and Sunday afternoons sweeping out Mr. Levine's bakery, that amazing part of my young life concluded when my family moved to the other side of town. I was sad when that part of my life came to an end. Mr. Levine had become really important to me when I was that young, skinny kid. He was, for me, teacher and mentor, wise man and counselor, source of peace and knowledge and wisdom.

I'm sure I didn't realize at the time that Mr. Levine had provided me with a basis for living that I would go back to over and over again throughout the years of my life. I don't think in the moment I was ever consciously aware of how influential he was, but over time I began to recognize that some of the things he told me as I swept out the bakery had become the foundation for a life worth living. When I strayed from that foundation, not too many years after my time with Mr. Levine, things did not go well. Not well at all.

There were a few years when I didn't reference any of the wisdom Mr. Levine had provided in that year and a half I spent at the bakery. After my stint in the Army, I ended up in New York, where, as people used to say, I fell in with the wrong crowd. I did lots of risky things, hung around with some pretty bad people and, worse, adopted their truths as my own. It became okay in my mind to consciously do the wrong thing.

For several years, I was not a person regular people would want to have anything to do with. It was a bad time, even though, like James Cagney in that old movie, I thought I was on top of the world. In reality, I was at the bottom of the heap. It was as if the part of my

Mr. Levine and Me

mind that had once been filled with the good words of a good man had shut down. Any barriers to destructive thought and behavior had fallen away, and I just did what I did with no regard for consequences. That is, until there were consequences. Eventually it all caught up with me and I ended up as a guest of the states of New York and New Jersey for about five years.

The time I spent on the inside was not horrible. Boring, yes, but horrible, no. Each day was exactly like the one that had preceded it and exactly like the one that would follow. Life was lived in accordance to when a bell rang. *A bell at wake-up time. A bell at meal time. A bell at work time. A bell at recreation time. A bell at lights-out time. And then, again, a bell at wake-up time..... Ad infinitum.* All that regimentation was a way of life, one that organized time with no effort on my part. It was all done for me and mandated.

I knew very quickly that I didn't want to end up like some of the people I met on the inside, the ones who came inside for a while, were released, and after a while returned with another stint in front of them. Some people followed that pattern their whole lives. I think they thought of their times of incarceration as simply part of the cost of doing business. I knew right away that was not a path I wanted to walk. One stint was more than enough for me. I promised myself when all of this was finished for me that it would never, ever be repeated.

While I was on the inside I finished high school. I had quit going to school at sixteen and enlisted in the Army at seventeen. I was proud of the GED certificate I earned while I was inside. I also learned how to run printing equipment, and I was lucky enough to work for a while as the clerk in the Jewish chaplain's office. The chaplain was a young rabbi who came in to lead a service each week, and to meet with inmates who had made appointments to see him about whatever was on their minds. He was a good and kind person. I never felt anything other than compassion from him. He wasn't judgmental and, I believe, he thought that each of the people who had gone astray was redeemable. Part of my reason for taking

An Aside

high school classes and working in the chaplain's office was because I thought it would be helpful with the parole board. It probably was, but both of those experiences turned out to be much more. They were like arrows pointing to a better path.

At some point after I was paroled from New York to my sentence in New Jersey, I was assigned to an outside detail riding in a large truck with another inmate and one of the officers, Mr. Seely, making deliveries to various institutions around the state. I did that work for about six months until, because I was considered by the authorities to be a model inmate, one who never caused any trouble and who followed all the rules, I was offered the opportunity to participate in a work-release program. Of course I accepted and I was moved out of the prison to a farm owned by the Department of Corrections.

There was a dairy operation there, and it was also the place where some of the trustees were housed. Every morning a person in civilian clothes picked me and a couple other men up and brought us to our work-release jobs. At the end of each workday someone else picked us up and returned us to the farm. My job was at an aluminum anodizing plant along a highway near East Brunswick, New Jersey. When I was finally paroled, I continued working there, rising to the level of foreman of the shipping department. It was because I worked there that I ended up getting to know, almost by accident, the rabbi of a nearby congregation, Isaac Moseson. He, like Mr. Levine from my childhood, recognized something in me and guided me toward what ultimately became my career as a cantor and rabbi. All those intersecting events turned out to be integral to my life moving forward. And as I once heard someone say, "Coincidences are the small miracles for which God takes no credit."

Now, more than fifty years after the events I've written about above, I'm retired, full of my years, and filled with memories of good times and bad times, happy and sad times, the people I've helped along the way, and the people I failed to help. Memories from childhood, young adulthood, middle age, and old age are blended together as if they are from the same moment. I know they

Mr. Levine and Me

are not, but when they come up in my thoughts, they are all, each of them, in the *right now*. Stephen King put it better than I could in one of his books, *Song of Susannah*: "In the Land of Memory the time is always *Now*. In the Kingdom of Ago, the clocks tick... but their hands never move. There is an Unfound Door (O lost) and memory is the key which opens it."

Something I should note here. As I said earlier, Legion Avenue and the shops and people and bakery that were such an important part of my stomping grounds back in the early 1950s were gone by the mid-1960s, victims of the urban renewal aspirations of that time. The bulldozers came, destroyed what had been a vibrant place filled with good people, and left a wasteland in its place.

The rest of the anecdotes in this book will continue to reflect upon the wisdom of that baker from my childhood on Legion Avenue.

If Somebody Needs Your Help, Help Them

For about six months, I spent my days on the truck with another inmate and the officer, Mr. Seely. First thing in the morning we loaded boxes of printed materials from the print shop, along with office machines and things like desks that were being moved from one institution to another. Sometimes we loaded canned goods and kitchen supplies or cleaning supplies. When we were finished loading we went and made deliveries to various state institutions, unloaded and sometimes loaded other things in place of what we dropped off. We were usually back inside the wall by mid-afternoon and free to do whatever we wanted the rest of the day. The next morning we did it again. It was what people called "Doing easy time." And it got even easier. After a month or so of working on the truck, the other inmate and I were moved to the farm, outside the "wall," about ten or so miles away. It was much better there.

One day as we were driving along on a rural road we saw a man on the shoulder frantically waving his arms. Mr. Seely stopped to see what was going on. I rolled down my window on the passenger side and heard the man shouting, "My brother's down in the hole! My brother's down in the hole!"

The three of us jumped out of the truck and followed the man to a spot near the road where there was a low cement structure that had an open manhole on the top. I got there first and looked down. There was a man at the bottom, about fifteen or twenty feet down,

Mr. Levine and Me

laying on his back. He looked unconscious. He wasn't moving. I started climbing down the steel ladder that was attached to the inner wall and shouted to whoever could hear, "Get a rope! Get a rope!" and continued climbing down. By the time I reached the bottom the other truckman had gotten a rope from our truck and dropped it down. I tied it into a loop and placed it under the unconscious man's arms and yelled, "Pull him up!" The people up top hauled the man up and I began climbing the ladder behind him, hanging on as best I could.

I started feeling weak as I went up. My breath was getting shallow. I felt like I was going to pass out. I was being overcome by whatever fumes had overcome the man who was being hauled up. I was about halfway up the ladder as the unconscious man was pulled through the opening above and I yelled as loud as I could for the guys on top to drop the rope to me. "I'm going to pass out. Drop me the rope!" The rope came down, fortunately still tied in a loop, and I was somehow able to get it around me and under my arms before everything went dark. When I awoke, I was laying on the grass next to the cement structure. The other man who had been hauled up was sitting nearby, awake now but looking pale and spent.

Mr. Seely had radioed for an ambulance and I heard the siren getting closer. When it arrived, one of the medical people put an oxygen mask on me and another on the other guy. In a few minutes we were both okay. The medics stuck around for fifteen or twenty minutes, and when they were sure we were all right they packed up their gear and left. Nobody had to be transported to a hospital. After the ambulance left, the man who had flagged us down explained that he and his brother were maintenance men who had had some work to do in that underground chamber. They hadn't followed the normal procedure of ventilating the chamber before going down, because they thought they'd be in the hole for just a few minutes. Whatever fumes had built up down there had rendered one of them unconscious, and the other was nearly out as he clambered up the ladder to safety. His brother (it really was his brother who worked with him) would certainly have died had we not come along just when we did. We sat around for a while drinking water and talking while Mr. Seely wrote an incident report. The brothers sealed up the underground chamber with its manhole cover and left. Then Mr. Seely, the other inmate and I climbed into our truck and went off to finish our day's work.

I had a parole hearing the following month in a conference room at the prison. The first question I was asked was about the incident along the road. The chairman asked me if I knew going down in the hole was a dangerous thing to do, and I told him I hadn't really thought about it at the time. He went on talking about my record of good behavior and my adherence to the rules. But he and one of the other members of the panel went back several times to what had happened on that rural roadway a month or so earlier. One of the people in front of me said, "You were a hero that day. Mr. Seely's report indicates that you saved a man's life." I fumbled for words and said I didn't think I was hero. Then the chairman told me we were finished, and I'd have the decision of the board the following week. I left, and the prison bus took me back to the farm. I was free for the rest of the day, free to wonder if I'd get good or bad news the following week. Other thoughts came to mind as well.

It had been about fifteen years since I'd left Legion Avenue. I had not seen Mr. Levine more than a couple of times during those years. He had become, by this time in my life, a memory of a time long ago. I knew he would not have liked the turns my life had taken, but I thought that, given who I remembered him to be, he would give me a chance to make things right, just as he had done the one time I lied to him when I was twelve years old.

An image of him appeared in my mind, and for a moment I was back in the bakery with my broom, sweeping up the flour. I saw Mr. Levine come through the door that led to the bakery. I stopped sweeping, and he told me there was a lady who needed a hand. I followed him into the store and there was this old woman just standing there, with a bag of rolls in her hand. Outside, I could see through

Mr. Levine and Me

the store window a child's red wagon with wooden-slatted sides filled with a few shopping bags full of groceries. Mr. Levine spoke to the woman and said, "Michael will help you with it." Then he told me to walk her home and carry her things upstairs for her. The woman smiled and thanked Mr. Levine and off we went.

When I returned to the store to finish sweeping, Mr. Levine thanked me for helping the lady with her bags. He told me I had done a "big mitzvah."

"You know why I asked you to help her out?" he said. I just looked at him and he continued, "Because she needed some help." He went on as he always did, saying, "Michael, I'm gonna tell you something, and I want you should remember it for the rest of your life. If someone needs your help, help them."

When I came out of my little reverie, I thought the old advice from Mr. Levine must have been lurking near the surface that day on the road. Maybe it was him, somehow, that prompted me to climb down into that underground chamber to help the poor guy laying there unconscious. I remembered thinking that day how I, when I was a kid, thought Mr. Levine was always right. I credited him for my having done the right thing that day.

The week passed, and I got the letter from the parole board. *Would I have to spend another year inside? Would I get a release date?* My hand was trembling as I opened the envelope. I unfolded the letter slowly, almost afraid to look at it. But there it was: I was going to be a free man in just one month. I knew I was at the end of my trouble time, and I vowed to never have such troubled times again. I thanked Mr. Levine in my thoughts many times over the next few days for somehow being with me. In some mystical way, I thought, when I needed some help, he helped me.

Whatever You Do Has Your Name on It

Two or three years after my family moved away from Legion Avenue, all that had changed was our location. Most everything else stayed the same. There was still never enough money. Morris still worked at the shoe store downtown and my mother still cashiered at the luncheonette on Whalley Avenue. It was a little easier for her because our new apartment was only a few blocks away from where she worked, so she didn't need a bus ride to get back and forth.

It got a little harder for my brother and me, though. When we moved we had to give up our paper routes, and my sweeping at the bakery ended too, partly because I was living pretty far away, and partly because Mr. Levine wasn't working at the bakery every day anymore. We had to find other things to do if we wanted to have any spending money. I was lucky enough to find a gas station that would let me pump gas and clean windshields now and then, and I sometimes delivered prescriptions on my bike for a nearby drug store. I didn't get paid for that, but almost everyone gave me a tip when I brought their medicines to them, and I could get a free milk shake or soft drink at the soda fountain in the drug store. When I was thirteen and celebrated my Bar Mitzvah I got quite a few money gifts, but I didn't get to keep much of that since my mother needed it to pay for all the food she provided for the gathering after the service. I remember vaguely that she complained about a few people putting pastries or lox and bagels into bags to take home.

Mr. Levine and Me

I still got down to Legion Avenue once in a while. I'd usually go with Morris to pick up our Sunday brunch stuff, along with all the newspapers. It was too far to walk, but my uncle Harry would sometimes take us there in his car. He was getting his Sunday brunch stuff too. We didn't go every Sunday though, maybe just once or twice a month. When we did go, we always stopped in to see Mr. Levine and buy some bagels. Sometimes, if he was there, I'd hang around with him while Morris did the shopping along the Avenue. That's pretty much the way it went for a couple years until I started high school and got a few "real" jobs. Things were the same, but things were also different.

When I was in the tenth grade I was lucky enough to get what they used to call "working papers." That meant I would be able to work after school, even though I was not yet sixteen. Someone at the school sent me to speak with the owner of a print shop, and he gave me an after-school job. Minimum wage back then, 1956, was one dollar an hour. I worked four afternoons each week, three hours each time, learning how to clean presses, and after a while I learned to operate a two-color offset press. I got paid twelve dollars a week. It felt like a lot of money to me. It was a lot more than I ever made delivering papers, or prescriptions, or sweeping the floor of the bakery. It cost just a half dollar to see a movie. I think popcorn was a dime, and just a nickel for a candy bar or a Coke. For the first time in my life I could buy some of my own clothes. It felt good to be wearing things no one else had ever worn. My work in the print shop ended at the end of tenth grade, because my job there was part of some program administered by my school. The following school year some other kid would be working at the print shop.

I remember something about working there that seemed at the time to be very important. It still seems very important. The process of getting a print job through the plant was pretty complicated. Quite a few people were involved in every job. A compositor and layout person, a camera man and plate maker, a stockroom person, a press operator, the shipping department. Each step of the work had

Whatever You Do Has Your Name on It

to be approved by whoever was responsible for that step. It was a way of assuring that each job lived up to the highest standard.

It usually worked out just right. One time, though, a job came through for some state agency. It was a letterhead order, thousands of copies printed on expensive linen paper. Everyone signed off on the job as it moved through the process. After it shipped out it was returned a couple weeks later because of a mistake. 'Connecticut' was misspelled as 'Connnecticut,' with three 'n's.' Everybody who worked on that job had approved every step, including the boss. Nobody spotted the error. Everyone's eyes saw 'Connecticut,' spelled correctly. The only thing the foreman said about it was, "When you think it's perfect, take another look, and I will too."

He wasn't angry. Sometimes things happen. Then he went to one of the big cutting machines and cut a stack of the letterheads into notepad size and told me and another after-school worker to make them all into note pads. "Someone will use them. Just make sure the printed side is down," he said.

He reminded me of Mr. Levine when he said that. My mind brought me back to the bakery. Mr. Levine was teaching me how to make those wonderful, knotted rolls out of challah dough. He showed me how to cut three and a half ounce chunks of dough with the scraper, let them rest a minute, roll them into round foot-long snakes, and then form the double knot and place them on a pan, separated enough so they wouldn't touch when they rose. If I made the knot incorrectly, Mr. Levine would tell me to do it again, and I would, over and over, until I got it right. "Remember," he said to me more than once during the time I spent with him, "whatever you do has your name on it."

Once I finished a whole pan and said, "Look, it's perfect." He looked at my work and said, "If you think it's perfect, it ain't." I think he was trying to get me to understand that nothing we do can be perfect. Good, yes. Excellent, also yes. But perfect?

And that reminds me of something that I remember from another time, many years later. My stepdaughter, Rebecca, was in college at

Mr. Levine and Me

Nebraska Wesleyan, the same university at which I was an adjunct professor. One of her professors, Dr. Peabody, was a colleague and friend. Rebecca was writing a paper for his class and had asked for several extensions. She was a good student and he knew she was not just making excuses, so he allowed her a few extensions. But when she asked for just one more, he said to her, "Sometimes finished is better than perfect." The foremen at the print shop, and Mr. Levine and the professor, were all, in a way, saying the same thing, the same message. There is no such thing as perfect.

When that school year was over and my work at the print shop came to an end, I got a summer job working for an electrician, Kaplan and Son. My job, Mr. Kaplan told me, was to be a "mule," a human pack animal lugging BX cable here and there and fetching anything the other workers might need. During the time I worked for Mr. Kaplan, he was wiring the houses in a new subdivision. All of the houses going up there were pretty much identical inside, with differences in siding or shingles on the outside. It was like the Levittowns that sprang up after World War II, originally meant to provide affordable housing options for returning veterans. The wiring in these houses was all the same. Each morning, a couple hours before the workers arrived, Mr. Kaplan and his son came and drilled all the holes through which cables would be pulled. In the basement of each house was a center beam, and when the Kaplans finished drilling the holes in each house they'd go and snap a blue chalk line on it. That was because when the workmen pulled their cables, Mr. Kaplan wanted the ones that would run down the center beam to the circuit breaker box to be stapled up straight, following the chalk line. He insisted on it.

One afternoon, just before quitting time, Mr. Kaplan gathered all of us together in one of the houses and had us go down to the basement. When we got there, he pointed to the center beam and asked who had worked in this house. A couple of the guys raised their hands like kids in school and Mr. Kaplan asked them, "What do you see?" One of the men said something like "Whaddya mean, I don't see nothin." Then Mr. Kaplan moved his hand along the cables on the center beam, following their wavy length, and said, "Well, I see a crappy job. Tear it down and do it over again, and this time do it right. Straight." The other guy made the mistake of saying, "They're pretty straight already. It's good enough." Mr. Kaplan, obviously not pleased, said "Rip those cables down and do it again. Straight. Or go home and don't come back again."

The first guy asked, "Why do you care if the cables are a little off the chalk line?" And I'll never forget this: Mr. Kaplan said, "Do it right. My name is on it." It's almost as if, at least in my memory, the foreman at the print shop and Mr. Levine, and Mr. Kaplan and Dr. Peabody, were different representations of the same person. They each passed along similar words of wisdom to guide me.

When you think it's perfect, take another look.
If you think it's perfect, it ain't.
Sometimes finished is better than perfect.
Do it right. My name is on it.
Remember, whatever you do has your name on it.

The words from those people and others like them have resonated with me time and time again. Whether I was working to make a living, doing homework when I was studying at seminary, leading a service, writing a eulogy or a sermon, preparing music for some special event, teaching a class at the university, landscaping around my house, planting my vegetable garden, making my favorite marinara sauce or baking bread each week, the words of Mr. Levine and other mentors who turned up sometimes to point the way come back to me. At such times I try to remember that whatever I do, my name is on it.

It Doesn't Matter Who the Other Guy Is.

I used to hang around with Bobby, Joey, and Ash Wednesday all the time. They were the ones I thought of as my best friends. We did everything together. We went to Edgewood Avenue Park and rode the bike paths there. We played touch football on the lot near the student nurses' dorm at St. Raphael's hospital. We ate in each other's homes. We'd get scolded by any, or sometimes all, of our parents. I went surreptitiously to their church sometimes, and they came to my synagogue. We all knew how to get a free pickle from Mrs. Goldstein, an apple from Mr. Kaplan, or a free cookie from Mr. Levine. We were constant companions.

I was never jealous of Bobby. He was pretty much like me. The same for Ash Wednesday. He was chubby and had that big mole on his forehead. But Joey? That was another story. I was always envious of him. He had all the qualities I wished I had. He was taller than me. He was strong. He was good at baseball (I always got stuck playing right field, where nothing much ever happened). Joey was sure of himself, and I was never sure of myself. Joey got the best grades in school. Everyone liked him and I always thought that everyone just put up with me. In my mind Joey could do anything he wanted to do, and I didn't even know what I wanted to do.

Sometimes I spoke with Mr. Levine about all the ways Joey was better than me. Mr. Levine always listened and maybe shrugged. One of those times I remember saying that I thought life would just

It Doesn't Matter Who the Other Guy Is.

be better if I could be more like Joey. Mr. Levine looked at me then with a serious expression on his face. "Michael," he said, "Do you like anything about yourself as much as you like everything about Joey?" I didn't respond right away. I had to think about it because it was hard to think of anything about myself that I liked better than just about anything about Joey. So I just kept talking about him.

"Joey is so cool," I said. "He can do anything." Joey this and Joey that.

Finally, Mr. Levine stopped me with a wave of his hand and said, "Okay, okay, enough about Joey, but what about you? What do you think about yourself? What's good about you?" I muttered something about how it would be better if I were more like my friend Joey. I couldn't think of anything about myself that even came close.

Mr. Levine looked at me for a minute or two. He still had that serious expression. I knew he was about to say something important. He always looked that way when he was about to tell me something he thought I needed to know. "Michael," he said, "I'm gonna tell you something and I want you should remember it for the rest of your life. It doesn't matter who the other guy is. It matters who you are."

I've thought about those words lots of times over the years. And you know? It really doesn't matter who the other guy is. The other guy does whatever he does. He's good at whatever he's good at. He's not good at whatever he's not good at. He does whatever he does and maybe it's good and maybe it's bad, maybe important and maybe trivial, maybe really great and maybe of no consequence at all. And none of that, not one iota of it, has anything to do with me, or with the arc of my life. He does what he does. I do what I do. And what I do is important. Nothing anyone else might do is more important in my life than anything I may be doing.

For most of my life I've been pretty unsure of myself, even though I've got a wall full of awards in my office from all sorts of different organizations. ACLU Civil Libertarian of the Year, Man of the Year from the NAACP, Ecumenical Person of the Year from the United Methodist Church, citations from the Borough President of Queens for interfaith work and presented to me during a Ramadan celebration. I received awards from the Suffolk County Executive and the City Council of New York. I was even presented with the Key to the City by Don Wesley, the then mayor of Lincoln, Nebraska.

All those folks thought there was something worthwhile about me. But none of that really matters to anyone but me. Joey from Legion Avenue, if he was still around, would not be affected by those plaques and citations hanging on my wall. His own accomplishments are what matter to him, and somehow define him, just as my own accomplishments matter to me. I've had some good ones, to be sure, but in reflection, I know they don't matter much. What really matters is my next steps, not the ones from yesterday or from long ago. *Which way am I heading?* That's important. And thinking of Mr. Levine I remind myself that the thing that really matters is not who the other guy is, but who I am.

Your Life Is the Only Story You Get to Tell

I remember once, long after moving away from Legion Avenue, spending an hour at the bakery one Sunday morning. Mr. Levine welcomed me, got me a cup of coffee, and sat with me at one of the tables by the front window of the store. It had been quite a while since I'd been there and it felt good to see him again. But it didn't feel good to see how my old neighborhood had deteriorated. Houses on some of the side streets were boarded up. Some of the stores I had gone into when I lived around there were empty, closed, and one that I noticed had broken, unrepaired windows. There were piles of trash here and there. The crowds of happy people doing some Sunday morning shopping were much smaller. It was a pretty sad place, and I was sad to see it. It had only been a few years, but the changes were enormous.

It was a sad time for me for another reason. I had come back to New Haven from Oklahoma, where I was stationed at Fort Sill, to attend the funeral of my stepfather, Morris. He had died on July 19, 1959. I got word of his death the next day and was able to arrange bereavement leave and travel the same day. I got to New Haven on the day of the funeral and took a cab from the railroad station downtown directly to the funeral home. I got there before the end of the service and went with my mother and sister to the little Jewish cemetery on Whalley Avenue for the burial. Many years later, my mother would be buried beside Morris. When we went back to my mother's apartment, I learned that Morris had taken his own life. I didn't know why he would have done that. It was inconceivable to me. Morris was strong and steady, always ready for anything.

As my mother tried to explain what had happened, I was struck by her lack of emotion. I didn't know she was trying to hide her sadness. Morris had really loved her and her children, David, Sylvia, and me. When Sylvia was married it was he who escorted her down the aisle, not our father, who was there but not part of the ceremony. I know Morris loved David and encouraged him with his love of music. He encouraged me, too, and forgave my misdeeds time and time again.

I began to understand, but never completely, why Morris had, in some terrible swirl of shame, committed suicide when I saw the collection of newspaper articles my mother had clipped from the local paper. One of the headlines read: "War Hero Arrested for Embezzlement." As best as I was able to figure out from the newspaper articles, Morris had caught his co-manager stealing from the till to cover his gambling debts. When Morris caught him he didn't want to have his co-manager arrested and so, instead, began having him slowly replace the money he had stolen. Morris helped by juggling the books so that, at least on the surface, things would look okay.

It might have worked, except for an untimely audit by the corporate office that exposed what was going on. Both Morris and his co-manager, Joe Grace, were arrested, their names smeared all over the papers. Morris was respected in the community, not for his wealth, because he didn't have any, but for his integrity, which he had in abundance. He had, for a while, been the president of his synagogue, for example. Knowing him as I did I was sure that, had he lived, he would never have gone there again. The shame of his arrest, the loss of his good reputation and the rest of it was more than he could bear. So he went to New York City, found his way to the Manhattan Bridge, and leaped to his death.

My mother showed me the note Morris had left. It read: "Dear Ann, Joe Grace is a bastard. Maybe we'll meet in a better place.

Love always, Morris." There was another newspaper article I didn't see until almost fifty years later, just after my mother died in 2007. It was among her things. The headline read: "Rubinsky Exonerated in Embezzlement Case." I didn't read the article.

I told the story of Morris to Mr. Levine that day in the bakery. He just listened. He didn't stop me with the usual wave of his hand. His eyes looked teary as I told him my sad story. After a while I stopped, and a long silence hung in the air between us. Finally Mr. Levine smiled a small smile and said, "Michael, you should know this: Morris had a good story. He was a good man. He lived a decent life. Maybe he made a mistake, like everyone. Maybe one day you'll know more of his story. I hope so. His life was a good life, and that's his only story. And that's the same with you. Your life is the only story you get to tell. Try to make it a good story by how you live. I wish Morris had told his story instead of what he did. You think about that, Michael."

Whatever I have done throughout the years of my life, no matter what it may be, is a piece of my life only. It's the same for everyone. Little by little, over the span of years, we all do multitudes of things. They pile up inexorably outside of any consciousness we may believe we have. The collection of our actions, our thoughts and aspirations, successes and failures, advances and retreats, all of it, every iota, are the stuff of the stories of our lives. At any moment in time we are, somehow, the sum total of the things we have done. The thoughts we have entertained, the good and the bad, the important and the banal, the happy and the sad, these are all pieces of our story lines. The collective experiences are all part of the portrait of who we are, and no one can paint that portrait for us. Only we ourselves can do that. How we present ourselves to the world is in no way dependent on any fictional account we may conjure up about our lives. Our life stories have nothing to do with anything any other person has done, nor with anything another person may think of us. Our story is our story, and no one can tell it except ourselves.

Mr. Levine and Me

Even though Mr. Levine didn't say these exact words, he said things like them, and when I think about things like this, the words often come to me in his voice. I hear him say, "You can lie about yourself. You can puff yourself up. You can pretend to be someone else. But it isn't possible to undo the story you've created about yourself over your lifetime. If you want to be thought of as an honorable person, live as an honorable person. If you want to be thought of as kind and charitable, do acts of kindness and charity. You can't just say you are honorable or kind or charitable. And remember that the truth will always, at some time or another, become clear. You have no control over that."

Your story is your story. It will always be your story. Your story will never be the story of any other person. You are unique and your story is likewise unique. You should take care with the way you write your story. The path you decide to walk will provide the vocabulary. It's your life, and your life is the only story you get to tell.

Nobody Can Make You Happy

I spent more time around Mr. Levine than any other adult. I saw my grandparents every so often. I used to love hanging out with my grandfather Michael. Sometimes in the summer he'd let me help out in his shop. He owned a small shop where custom-made suit jackets, or "coats" as he called them, got their first pressing. Sometimes he sent me a few blocks away to one of the tailors who had their shops near the Yale campus to pick up or deliver some coats. Other times I'd run the wet canvas cloths through the wringer. That's what he, and my uncle Harry, who worked with him in the shop, used to produce the steam that was needed for the pressing. I remember my grandfather's iron was sixteen pounds and my uncle's was eleven. Those big irons had gas hoses connected to them and a flame burning inside. My grandfather could run his iron down a sleeve and catch it midair to bring it back the other way with his other hand. His forearms would have done Arnold Schwarzenegger proud.

Sometimes I'd go with my grandfather on a summer afternoon to watch the Italian old guys playing bocce. All of those old guys, my grandfather included, bet on the games and they had a good time doing it. I had a good time just being with my grandfather. My uncle Harry sometimes took me fishing with my cousins, Gregory and Loren. We went to Stevenson Dam on the Housatonic River a few times and fished at Lake Zoar, and I remember being excited any time I caught a fish. It was always too small to eat and we threw it back into the water, but it was exciting to catch it anyway. Of course my grandmother Sophie was an important part of my young life too. She taught me some of the basics of cooking and always had some of those Ukrainian hard filled candies around. At home, my mother always seemed tired from her long work days, and Morris was such an avid baseball fan that sometimes he would watch one game on television and go back and forth between it and a radio in the kitchen to listen to another game. They were both good to me, but I hardly ever got to talk about things with them. They were either too tired or too busy.

Mr. Levine was different. I shared everything with Mr. Levine during the year and a half I spent my afternoons sweeping the bakery. Wanting to be someone else, being jealous, being sad, being happy or angry. The whole gamut of emotions was on full display with him. I didn't realize it, or even think about it at the time, but Mr. Levine knew more about me than my brother or sister, or even my mother or stepfather, or my grandparents or uncles or aunts. He was the one I trusted with everything. No matter what I was grumbling about, he was willing to listen, at least for a little while. He was more than family and more than counselor. He was my source of wisdom, even if I didn't know it then.

Sweeping out that bakery and talking with Mr. Levine were so very important to me. I may have thought they were important because of the quarter I got every day. But later, much later actually, I came to realize they were important because of the path they helped me to lay out for myself later in life, a path I couldn't have followed without the navigation tips that came my way from Mr. Levine.

I remember when I won my bicycle for selling the most Boy Scout Jamboree tickets. I rode that beautiful Raleigh English bicycle over to the bakery to show it off to Mr. Levine. Of course he had been the key to my great win because he told me a good way to sell a lot of tickets. He looked my new bike over approvingly and said, like any Jew in those days might have said, "Use it in good health." I was gushing all over myself about how happy winning that bike made me feel, and Mr. Levine stopped me and said, "Do you think winning that bicycle is what makes you happy?"

I said I was sure winning the bike made me happy.

"Are you really sure?" he asked. "I'm gonna tell you something and I want you should remember it for the rest of your life. Nothing can make you happy. No one can make you happy. And also nothing and nobody can make you sad."

I didn't understand. I won the bike. I was happy. But Mr. Levine continued, repeating himself, "Nobody can make you happy and nobody can make you sad. Only you can do that."

As was often the case with Mr. Levine's words, they didn't hit home right away, but sometimes, years later, they came back. His words were sometimes like a manual for living that was somehow stored away in my brain. When I needed them, there they were. When they emerged they sometimes set off a torrent of thoughts and gave me the solution to some problem I'd never confronted before.

I think everyone has said something like, "You make me happy," or "That makes me sad." When we say things like that I'm sure we mean them. The only trouble, at least according to Mr. Levine, is that it isn't true. Being happy is a choice. Being sad is also a choice. Mr. Levine's words about this and about many other things have stayed with me.

All through my professional life I've been asked to give my advice about lots of different things. Sometimes, and maybe even often, the advice I've given is the same advice I received many years before from Mr. Levine.

I remember that once a very sad woman came to my office at the synagogue. She wanted to talk with me about a friend who had unexpectedly died. One day her friend was there and the next she was gone. I listened as this sad person poured out her heart. She regretted that she hadn't seen it coming. She felt anger that her friend hadn't let her know what was going on.

Quite a few times during that conversation, the woman said she felt anger toward her friend's family and even toward her now dead friend as well. She was angry and she was sad. "They make me so mad," she said. "It makes me so sad that my friend is gone, that I'll never see her again. I'm angry I couldn't be with her when she needed me. Why did they do this to me?" I tried to explain that I thought her friend and her friend's family probably didn't want to burden anyone with the problems they were trying to deal with. Tears were coming down the woman's face as she told me her story. I listened and listened. I thought it was good that she was getting it off her chest.

Mr. Levine came to mind at some point and I began to speak as if I were somehow him. "Are you sure her family made you mad? Are you really angry at your friend? Do you really believe they did something to you?" We looked at each other in silence for a while before I spoke again. "Being happy is a choice and so is being sad. So is being angry."

We continued talking for a long time that day. When someone we care about dies, of course we feel sadness. But is it the death of the person that makes us sad? Or is it because we know that all the good moments and all the bad moments we shared with that person won't be happening anymore? But, with all the memories of our friend swirling about, maybe instead of feeling sad we might take the opportunity to revisit the relationship that was. Because, even in the face of death, that relationship can still endure. We can choose to remain sad, depressed, and angry, or we can embrace the memory of the time we shared. We can place ourselves in the presence of the one who is gone from our sight but still present in our hearts.

None of the things that happen at such times make us sad or happy. We ourselves are in control of the emotions we allow to rise. We can choose to drown in the sorrow of remembering bad times or what we perceive to be the failings of people who didn't keep us informed, or we can remember the good times we shared along the way. All the memories, of good and of bad, are there. We can do with them whatever we wish. That's our choice. And maybe we can remember that it's not really the passing of a friend that makes

Nobody Can Make You Happy

us sad, but more the choices we make as we deal with the death of that friend. Of course it's appropriate to be sad at such a time, but it's also appropriate to temper the sadness we allow to well up with the happiness we allowed to well up when we were with our friend in life.

These ideas that came to me from that old Legion Avenue baker when I was a young boy ring true to me now that I'm an old man myself. *Nobody makes you mad. Nobody makes you happy. Nobody makes you sad. Only you can do that.*

You are in charge of those things.

We cheat ourselves of our own reality when we assign responsibility for our emotions to others. It isn't easy to understand that we are responsible for our own emotional well-being and emotional turmoil, but it's still important to recognize that circumstances are not the culprit, but rather the springboard to decision making.

I'll always remember, even if I don't always put them into practice, the words of Mr. Levine when he told me, "Nobody can make you happy and nobody can make you sad."

If You Hide Who You Are, You're Nobody

I think the earliest memory I have was from when I was maybe four years old. We lived in a rented house on Greenwood Street then. There was a pear tree and an apple tree in the backyard. I know from family lore that my mother was working then at a nice restaurant, the Tivoli, as a waitress. My father was already out of the picture and it wouldn't be long before my brother, my sister and I would be placed in the orphanage while my mother got back on her feet after she and my father divorced.

It was sometime before D Day, although I didn't know anything about that at the time. It was night and we were at home. The radio was on. Other than that, it was quiet. My sister, Sylvia, was probably doing schoolwork, and my brother and I were laying on the floor listening to the radio. We used to listen to *The Lone Ranger*, *The Green Hornet*, or *The Shadow*. (I still remember the introduction to the last show: "What evil lurks in the heart of man? Who knows? The Shadow knows.")

That's how we spent most evenings until my mother got home from her job at the restaurant at about nine thirty each night. When my mother got home that evening, we all sat down at the table. My mother had a bite to eat, and Sylvia brought out whatever was for dessert that day. We always waited to have dessert until my mother came home.

If You Hide Who You Are, You're Nobody

Suddenly there was a loud banging at the door. My mother went and opened it and a man wearing a white helmet with the letters CD on each side of it came in. I learned sometime later that 'CD' stood for Civil Defense. He spoke in a loud but not angry voice. He knew us and we knew him because the CD people were all neighborhood volunteers.

"Ann," he said, "You have to pull your drapes. There's light getting out."

That's what they did during the war years. No lights. Car headlights were taped over. Windows had to be blocked on the inside. They were afraid the Nazis would somehow see the lights when they came to attack, if they came to attack. They never did, but Long Island Sound was only a few miles away, so who knows? The point is, people were told—instructed—not to make their presence known.

My mother apologized and dutifully pulled the draperies across the windows. The CD helmet guy waved goodbye and said one of those wartime catch phrases: "Loose lips sink ships. We can't let them know anyone's here," as he walked out the door.

Somehow, that relates to another early memory from a few years after that. The war was over, and now the world knew the Nazis had targeted, rounded up, sent to concentration camps, and ultimately murdered *en masse* Roma, (often referred to as "Gypsies"), homosexuals, disabled people, people with mental illnesses, and others, especially Jews, during their reign of terror. Now the war was indeed over, and the Nazis were defeated. People started to get back to life as it was before. But it was never the same again. The residue of hatred remained a part of the landscape. It didn't just go away.

I have a memory from a time when my grandparents came out to Guilford to visit with us and their old friends, Nicola and Katherine, the people who owned the chicken farm where we lived once Morris and my mother married. It must have been about 1947. The conversation around the table turned to the war, to the Six Million, to the greatest tragedy that had ever befallen the Jewish People. I remember how serious everyone was that day. They were still almost in a daze about what had happened during the war. At some point Nicola, who we always called Uncle Nick, turned to me and my brother David and said, "Never tell anyone you're Jewish." That was it. He didn't explain why he said that, but even though I was only about six years old and my brother seven and a half, we understood that he had said something important. From that day I knew I was not supposed to be who I was sometimes. The conversation around the table continued as cards were shuffled for a game of pinochle.

Even at that young age I knew there were people who didn't like Jews. When I was older and I knew more about what had happened to the Jews of Europe, I couldn't believe that despite those terrible things, there were still people who hated Jews. I guess it made sense to warn a Jewish kid to keep that part of who he was to himself. Uncle Nick's words haunted me for a long time, and for years I didn't tell people, especially people I didn't know, that I was Jewish. When we moved back to New Haven a few years after Uncle Nick told us to keep our Jewish identity to ourselves, that is what I did most of the time. I was a Jewish kid, but at the same time I wasn't. I've thought sometimes that it was because of that advice from Uncle Nick that very few of my friends as I grew up were Jewish. I think maybe I gravitated toward the Italian kids in the neighborhood and tried to be like them because it was somehow better to be like them than who I actually was.

I had some friends who knew I was Jewish. Bobby, Joey, and Ash Wednesday didn't care about things like that. And I know my grandparents had friends in the Ukrainian community who were not Jewish, and they didn't care about it either. But every now and then I'd hear something that reminded me of Uncle Nick's warning. People sometimes said they "Jewed him down" if they made a good deal on something. I heard people say that the Jews killed Jesus, and even though that didn't make any sense to me, it scared me when I heard it. I even heard, once or twice, that "Hitler didn't

If You Hide Who You Are, You're Nobody

go far enough with the Jews. He should have finished the job." So, I kept anything about being Jewish pretty much to myself. Uncle Nick must have been right.

Once, when I was at the bakery and had finished with my sweeping, I talked about antisemitism with Mr. Levine. I didn't call it antisemitism; I don't know if anyone used that word back then. Before I started that conversation, I asked Mr. Levine if he was Jewish. I didn't know for sure, even though I sometimes heard him speak Yiddish with some of the customers who came into the store. He told me he was Jewish, but not religious. And he was proud of being a Jew. "You know, Michael, we've been around for maybe five or six thousand years. No one else can say that." I asked him if he knew why people hated us and he said he didn't know why. He knew it didn't make any sense, but sometimes people are good at making no sense. Then he gave me a little history lesson.

"Did you know that about twenty-five hundred years ago, the Babylonians conquered us and sent a lot of our people into exile We survived that. And think about this—have you ever met a Babylonian? No, you haven't. There are no Babylonians anymore. But have you ever met a Jew?" He smiled and pushed the plate of cookies toward me.

I told Mr. Levine that day that I didn't tell most people I was Jewish. I didn't want anyone to know because I knew lots of people hated Jews. He looked serious, lines across his brow and eyes narrowed. "Michael," he said, "do you know some Italians?"

I told him I did and that he knew my best friends, Bobby, Joey, and Ash Wednesday, were Italian.

"Do you know that when Italians started coming to this country, a lot of people who were already here hated them, called them names, made up bad things about them. They weren't Jews," he said. "But that's how they were treated. Do you think they hid who they were? No, they kept their ways from the old country, spoke Italian to each other, kept their music and the way they cooked and the closeness of their families. Most of all they let everyone know they were Italians and proud of it. You like them and I like them, too. But most of all I respect them for who they are because they respect themselves for who they are.

"And you know," he said, "they respect me too, and not just for my bread and rolls, but because they know that I know who I am. And you know who you are too. You are a Jew. You will always be a Jew. Stand up and be proud you are a Jew. Your friends know they are Italian, and they are proud of that even if they never speak of it. You know you are a Jew. Be proud of that. Respect yourself just like your friends respect themselves.

"And Michael, one more thing, and I want you should remember it for the rest of your life: If you hide who you are, you're nobody."

Spend Some, Save Some, Give Some Away

After I had been sweeping the bakery for six or seven months I got in the habit of hanging around for a while, especially on Sunday afternoons, when I got finished. At first, I think it was because when I sat out in the store at one of the tables near the front window, Mr. Levine would give me a couple of cookies. It was like an extra reward on top of the quarter he gave me each day that I did the sweeping. On those afternoons Mr. Levine would spend a few minutes, or sometimes more, talking with me about different things. Over time, I came to enjoy those times with him. He always had something to tell me, and his words somehow embedded themselves in my memory. Even if I sometimes didn't understand them when he said them, they somehow reappeared later in life when I needed them. It's almost as if my young brain became a safekeeping place for the things he told me, locked most of the time, but open when needed.

One Sunday, when I had finished sweeping the bakery, I came into the store. Mr. Levine was busy putting loaves of bread, rolls, and bagels that hadn't sold into big bags. When I asked him what he was doing, he told me that he always took the leftovers to a church on Dixwell Avenue, where they had a food center for poor people. He said he did that every day. "Poor people have to eat, too," he said. We talked about that for a while, and I learned that the people who get that bread would never know it came from him.

Mr. Levine and Me

I remember he asked me if I had ever heard of Maimonides. I told him I'd heard the name before at Hebrew school, but I didn't know much about him. He explained that Maimonides was one of our great scholars who lived in Spain in the twelfth century, a long time ago. One of the things he taught was that one of the best ways to give to the needy is when the one who gives doesn't know who received and the one who receives doesn't know who gave.

"If someone who gets some of that bread sees me on the street and thought I knew they were getting some of my bread, they might be embarrassed about their need," Mr. Levine said. "And if I saw someone that I knew got some of that bread, I might be tempted to think I'm better than they are. It's better if neither of us knows."

Mr. Levine pointed to a shelf on the wall behind the cash register. There were a half dozen or so little metal coin boxes there. I recognized them because they were just like the ones on a shelf in my grandma Sophie's kitchen. I knew what they were for. Every so often they would be dropped off empty by one of the *schnorrer's*, or charity collectors, and then picked up later when they were full of coins and replaced with an empty one. The money collected went to various causes, depending on which of the schnorrer's the box had come from (my grandmother explained that to me once).

Mr. Levine said the boxes (*pushkes*, he called them) were the same as the bread. He sometimes put his spare change in them, or customers would tell him to put some of the change they had coming to them into the boxes. They would not know who was helped by their gifts, and the ones who were helped would not know who helped them.

It wasn't until I was many years older that I learned that the word we use in Hebrew to mean charity, *tzedakah*, doesn't mean charity at all, at least not in the way we usually think of it. Tzedakah means something like righteousness or justice. I learned at some point when I was older that the English word 'charity' comes from the Latin *caritas* and means something like "from the heart." In

Spend Some, Save Some, Give Some Away

other words, it means to give voluntarily. You do some charitable act because you feel like doing it.

The Jewish idea of charity is that it's not voluntary but rather mandated. We're supposed to look after the widow and the orphan and the poor who live among us. Doing charitable acts is, according to Judaism, an obligation. Voluntary giving is also good, but since it's not required it's not as powerful as tzedakah, which is.

I asked Mr. Levine why he did this, since he had told me once that he was Jewish, but not religious. I remember he told me that you don't have to be religious to be human. You can always do the right thing, religious or not, and you can live up to high standards without praying all the time. He went on that day, more than usual.

"Michael," he said, "I'm lucky enough to make a pretty good living. I can afford to eat every day and live in a good place. I always remember something my mother, her memory is for blessing, told me back in the old country. She told me that if I had some money that I should spend some, save some, and give some away. Every time I give some away, a little or a lot, her words are in my mind. I see her as if she was there with me, reminding me to do the right thing."

Not too long ago, a couple of years for one and about six months for the other, my granddaughters Elise and Marin became bat mitzvah. It was an important day for them, and for me and the rest of the family as well. We were all so very proud of what they had accomplished. The gift I gave to each of my granddaughters was the same. I wrote them each a letter that contained, among other things, some of what Mr. Levine taught me seven decades prior. At the end of each of their letters, I mentioned that the money I included with the letter was their gift and that they should spend some, save some, and give some away. I, without really thinking about it, had passed a few words from Mr. Levine along to them. I hope one day they will pass his words along to their children and grandchildren. If they do, he will live on long after I'm gone.

Being Afraid Sometimes Is a Good Thing

It was a beautiful, sunny day. Spring was here, and the rainy month of April was over. It was May 4, 1953, the day before my twelfth birthday. In just a month and a half, my first year of junior high school would be over. I already knew I was going to have a straight-A report card because all my teachers had complimented me on the progress I had made since my awful beginning in the first semester, when I had earned four Cs and a D. Most of my teachers had already told me I was going to get an A in their class if I completed all my assignments. I couldn't wait until I got that report card so I could show it off to everyone, especially Mr. Levine.

That Monday, school ended at 2:15 for me. There was study hall that day, and since I was all caught up on my homework I was able to talk my homeroom teacher into letting me leave early. Maybe she let me go early because I was doing so well that semester. I thought about that a little, but whatever the reason, I was happy about it. I wanted to be outside. I think the teachers would have liked to skip out as much as I did.

I stopped at a little store that was near the school and bought a candy bar to eat along the way. It wasn't a very long walk from my school to the neighborhood, and I wasn't in a rush. I picked up pebbles every now and then and threw them across the street, finished up my candy bar, and made my way, slowly, to Legion Avenue. I had to sweep the bakery but I couldn't start until after three, when

Being Afraid Sometimes Is a Good Thing

the bakers left for the day. When I got to Legion Avenue, it was not yet three o'clock. So I sat for a while on the bench in front of the luncheonette that had no name and watched the people go by for a little while.

At about three fifteen I got up and walked to the bakery, a block away. When I got there I was surprised to see a picture of Mr. Levine taped to the inside of the window. Someone had placed a sign beside it that read "Keep Him in Your Prayers." I ran into the store to find out what was going on. The first person I saw was Joe Yussel. Even though I was always a little afraid of him since the time he had shoved me after my broom hit his foot, I tugged at his sleeve.

"What's wrong with Mr. Levine?" I shouted. Joe Yussel didn't swat my hand away. He looked at me and touched the top of my head. "Michael, Mr. Levine is at St. Raphael's. He had a heart attack. They took him there this morning."

I asked Joe Yussel if he was going to be okay. I knew about heart attacks. People died from heart attacks. Joe Yussel, as kind as I'd ever seen him, said, "No one knows yet. We're just praying that he'll be all right. You pray too, Michael. He loves you."

Tears were flowing down my face. There was nothing I could do, and I knew it. I loved him too. Mr. Levine couldn't die. He was old, but not old enough for that. I went in the back, crying my head off, got my broom and swept the bakery. I knew I wouldn't be getting a quarter that day, and I also knew that I wanted the bakery to be perfect when Mr. Levine came back. When I finished I ran home and got my bike. I rode as fast as I could down Legion Avenue to Scranton Street and up George Street past the back of the nurses' dormitory and up Sherman Avenue to Chapel Street and the hospital. I left my bike in front of the hospital, not even thinking someone might steal it, and went inside.

When I got to the desk I asked where Mr. Levine was. The woman behind the desk asked for his full name. I knew it because he had told me what it was not long before.

"David Levine," I answered.

Mr. Levine and Me

"Why is he in the hospital?"

"He had a heart attack this morning," I said.

Then she asked me a question I knew I had to lie about. "Only family is allowed to visit. Are you family?"

Mr. Levine was as much my family as anyone in my real family, so I said with a straight face, "Yes. He's my grandfather. I have to meet my mother here."

The woman behind the desk gave me a little piece of paper with the room number written on it and pointed me to the elevator. "Go to the third floor," she said, and off I went.

I found Mr. Levine's room and went in. There he was, laying in the bed under a blanket. He looked so pale, so weak, so frail. Tears began to well up, but I somehow held them back. When Mr. Levine saw me he smiled a little and gestured that I should come closer. I sat down on the chair beside the bed and asked him if he was okay. He didn't answer my question. Instead he said he was happy to see me. He thanked me for coming to see him. I didn't know what to say, so I just sat there trying not to cry.

After a long silence, just sitting there looking at each other, Mr. Levine spoke. "Don't worry, Mikhail," he said, using the Ukrainian form of my name. "I'm going to be okay. I lived a good life, the life I wanted to live. I'm seventy-five years old this year, you know. Don't worry."

I didn't know he was that old until that moment. "I want you to be okay," I said.

He smiled that wan little smile again, but didn't say anything. After a little while he said he was feeling tired and wanted to get a little sleep before the nurse came back to check up on him. I stood up and he reached out and took my hand in his. "Don't worry," he said again. "I'll be okay." I said I would say a prayer for him, and he smiled.

He let go of my hand and I turned to leave. When I got to the door he said, "Did you sweep the bakery?" I told him I did, and he said he'd pay me when he got back to work. Then I said goodbye and walked out of his room.

I cried as I went down on the elevator. When I got outside my bicycle was still there where I left it, and I rode back to Legion Avenue and went home. It was after five when I got there. My mother asked where I had been, and I told her. She said that was too bad about Mr. Levine. "Such a nice man," she said. And then she asked me what kind of cake I wanted for my birthday, which was the following day.

My mother always baked whatever kind of cake my brother, my sister or I wanted for our birthdays. I thought for a minute and then told my mother I didn't want a cake. She said, "Of course you do. It's your birthday." And I said, "No Mom, not until Mr. Levine gets out of the hospital." She didn't try to convince me. I went into the room I shared with my brother and closed the door. I was glad my brother wasn't home.

I went to St. Raphael's each afternoon that week after I finished sweeping the bakery. Each day Mr. Levine looked a little better. He told me he called the ambulance himself when he started having pain and pressure in his chest. I asked him if he had been scared, and he told me he was afraid when it started to happen. "It was a heart attack," he told me. "If I hadn't been scared I would have never called for help, and I might have died there in the bakery. Being afraid is why I'm still here. Sometimes it's good to be afraid," he said. "It means you're smart." After we talked a little more, Mr. Levine asked me if I had swept the bakery. He asked that each day that I visited with him.

He told me everyone from the bakery had been up to see him, and a few of the people he knew from Legion Avenue had come too. He pointed at a couple of flower arrangements on the windowsill. He didn't mention family coming to see him, and so, since I always wanted to know but never had the guts to ask before, I said, "What about your family? Have they been up to see you?"

Mr. Levine and Me

Mr. Levine looked at me for what seemed like a long time. Finally he spoke quietly and said, "There is no family. I was married a long time ago. I loved my wife very much. We were going to have the best life anyone ever had. We were married for five years and a half when she was hit by a car. She died that day. We didn't have children. I never looked at another woman. I've missed my Kateryna every day of my life. She's the one I loved and I still love her." And then, "Please Michael, I don't want to talk about this now." I didn't ask again. I was afraid to. And I remembered what Mr. Levine had said a couple days earlier. "Sometimes it's good to be afraid. It means you're smart."

Mr. Levine was back at the bakery that Sunday when I got there to sweep the floor. He looked a lot older than before, even though just a week had gone by. I asked him if he was okay, all better, and he said, "I'm here, ain't I?" We didn't talk about his heart attack or his wife anymore. I was smart enough to never bring those things up again.

When I went home that Sunday, I walked into the apartment and said to my mother, "German Chocolate." She smiled.

78

Never Say I Love You Unless You Know What You're Talking About

Following my discharge from the Army and what I think of, not so lovingly, as my "trouble time," I spent a lot of time on West 45th Street in Manhattan. It was a pretty grubby place at the time, beginning in 1960 and over the next couple of years. My hangout of choice was the Wagon Wheel Bar, and that was where I met the people I ended up thinking of as my circle of friends. There was Sally and Chloe, two girls from the Midwest somewhere who turned up on the block one day and stuck around for a few months. Sally was plain looking, chubby and always smiling and laughing about something or other, and Chloe was, as I heard a couple of people say about her, drop dead gorgeous. Everyone loved Sally. Chloe, not so much. There was also Eli, the Jewish guy who wanted desperately to be Italian. He always dressed like a made man: suit and tie, perfectly folded handkerchief in the pocket of his jacket, dark hair slicked back in the style of the day, and a fedora on his head if he was outside. Of course there was "Schoolboy" Tarver. He was a large, middle-aged Black guy, always sharply dressed, with the shiniest wingtips there ever were. His nickname, Schoolboy, was because he always had a few books and a briefcase with him. Philosophy, fiction, history. Anytime he sat in the old Knickerbocker Hotel coffee shop holding court he would be reading one of his books, interrupted only by the steady stream of losers coming in to give him money for the nickel bags of heroin he had stashed in his brief case. One person I met was a guy named Al Pajou. He was from Boston, and he was always flush with cash. He and I ended up, after a while, doing some things together that didn't turn out so well, for me at least.

Another person I got to know back then was Victoria Cooper. She was doing a semester of study at one of the colleges in New York. Why she started hanging around on 45th Street is a mystery to me. She was pretty, with curly red hair and a face full of freckles that let you know she was Irish, except she wasn't Irish, but Scottish. I liked everything about her. She was not only pretty, but smart, too. I knew she was smarter than me because she, like Schoolboy, was always reading something (I hadn't seriously looked at a book since I decided to drop out of high school when I was sixteen). Victoria also had a beautiful lilting accent when she spoke, the kind that Americans always think of as sophisticated or intellectual. She had everything, I thought, except me. As much as I wanted to, I couldn't get up the courage to ask her out for quite a long time. I'm pretty sure she knew I was involved in some not-so-good stuff and I didn't want to risk the rejection I was sure would come from her if I asked her out. But every time I saw her, I knew I wanted to.

I knew a guy, Jerome, or "Jerry" as we called him, who worked as a doorman at the Metropole Cafe on Seventh Avenue, just up the way from the big billboard advertising Castro Convertible sofa beds. That night club was a famous place, and you couldn't get in without a reservation. I told Jerry about Victoria and that I was going to ask her out for New Year's Eve. I asked if he could get me in. He wasn't really that good of a friend, just someone I knew, but he told me he'd get me in if I greased his palm a little. I agreed. It was the middle of December, 1960, and New Year's Eve on Times Square was just a couple weeks off.

The day after I talked with Jerry I asked Victoria if she'd like to go to the Metropole with me for New Year's Eve. She looked at

Never Say I Love You Unless You Know What You're Talking About

me with a look that said, "Yeah, right." I'm sure she didn't believe I would get us into the Metropole. The Metropole Cafe was a famous jazz venue then. Jazz legends like Dizzy Gillespie and Gene Krupa sometimes played there. She couldn't believe I could get a reservation for New Year's Eve. But after a while I convinced her that I really had one, and if she didn't want to go with me, I was sure someone else would, although I'd much rather it be her. So we planned to meet up at nine on 45th Street at the Wagon Wheel and then walk over to the Metropole, just a couple blocks away.

On New Year's Eve we met at the Wagon Wheel as planned and walked over to the Metropole. I was wearing slacks and a dress shirt and tie with a blue blazer that had a nicely folded handkerchief in the pocket, just like Eli. Even though it was pretty cold I wasn't wearing a topcoat. It wasn't snowing at all, and the sky was clear. It was a good night for the Times Square celebration. Victoria looked great in a beautiful blue clinging dress that matched her eyes. I helped her put on her long, dark-blue coat. I felt like a gentleman. I had already let my friend Jerry know what time we would be coming to the Metropole, and when we got there he walked over to us and shook my hand like I was some kind of big shot and escorted us into the club. I handed him a twenty-dollar bill, and I felt certain Victoria noticed me doing that.

We had a really nice evening. Dinner, a few glasses of wine, great music, a little dancing, and then, at the stroke of midnight, there was a drumroll and the band began to play Auld Lang Syne. Everyone in the place was singing along, glasses held high. When that was finished, Victoria and I, like everyone else in the place, wished each other a happy New Year, embraced, and enjoyed a most wonderful kiss. We laughed as we went back to our table. I couldn't take my eyes off her. After an awkward bit of silence, I said, "Victoria, I think I love you." She looked at me for a moment and then said, "Michael, how can you say that. You don't even know me. We're just having fun."

After a little while we left the Metropole. The crush of people who had been on Seventh Avenue earlier had thinned out quite a bit. We walked about a block and I flagged down a taxi for Victoria. We hugged for a moment, she kissed me on the cheek, and then she got in the cab. I continued walking and stopped in the Wagon Wheel for a while. Eli and a couple of others I knew were still there even though it was about one in the morning by then. We talked for a few minutes and then I took a cab home to my apartment down on Seventh Avenue. I had visions of what it might have been like if Victoria Cooper had been going there with me. I told her I loved her, and she said I didn't even know her, so how could I say that? Victoria and I saw each other a few times over the next couple of months. Nothing was ever said about the end of that New Year's Eve date. We both acknowledged that we had a good time that night, and that was it.

Victoria eventually moved back to Scotland to be with her family. I've thought about her once in a while over the years and remember well the New Year's Eve when I told her that I thought I loved her. I hope she's had a happy life. I'm sure she has.

Once, when Victoria Cooper came into my memory years after that fateful New Year's Eve, a memory of Mr. Levine that really had nothing to do with me appeared. There was a guy who worked at the bakery. He was maybe thirty years old. He was a burly, muscular man, about five foot ten with a happy, round face. The feature I remember most about his looks was his entirely bald head. There was not a hair on it. I don't know if he was naturally bald or if he was way ahead of his time and had shaved his head. Not many people did that back then, unless maybe they were in the Marine Corps and had no choice about it. I never knew this baker's real name because the only thing I ever heard anyone call him was Curly.

Curly worked every day with Joe Yussel and Mr. Levine. Early in the morning they would make big batches of dough and let it rise in the proof boxes until it was ready to be formed into bagels. That's what they made first in the bakery. The three of them would

Never Say I Love You Unless You Know What You're Talking About

form the dough into bagels by hand (there were no bagel making machines back then). Curly or Joe Yussel would boil the risen bagels in a giant pot for about thirty seconds and then place them on boards that had been covered with burlap and soaked in a barrel of water overnight. Each of those boards was long enough to hold a half dozen bagels. I think the bagels got a quick egg wash before they went into a hot oven. The moisture in the boards and the burlap made the steam that created that semi-hard outer surface so familiar to bagel lovers. This went on until they made whatever amount was needed for orders and for sale in the store. I don't know how many dozens, but a lot, for sure. When that was finished, they moved on to rolls, various kinds of breads, cookies, and other sweet things. They kept at it until three in the afternoon and began again the next morning at four a.m.

One Sunday afternoon when I finished sweeping I went out to the store, where I expected my daily allotment of cookies and, of course, my quarter. When I got there Mr. Levine gave me a couple of cookies and a glass of milk and a quarter, as he did every day. I sat down at the table by the window and expected Mr. Levine to come and talk with me for a while. That's what usually happened, but this day was different. Just as I sat down Curly came into the bakery. He smiled at me as he strode over to the counter and said something like, "Hey, that's a good job you do in there. The place always looks good when I get here." That felt good. I didn't know anyone noticed except Mr. Levine.

Curly began talking to Mr. Levine. He spoke in his regular voice so I was able to hear him. "David," he said, "I need some advice." I didn't know Mr. Levine gave other people advice. I suppose I thought I was the center of his universe or something. Curly went on and Mr. Levine listened, just like he did with me. "I've been seeing that girl Annemaria, you know, the one who comes in sometimes to say hello. I'm definitely falling for her. When I'm with her I feel happy all the time, and I think she feels the same way. What do you think?"

Mr. Levine and Me

Mr. Levine looked pretty serious and didn't speak for a while. Finally he said, "What do I think about what?" Curly looked surprised and said, "What do you think about Annemaria?" Mr. Levine responded, "Annemaria? I think she's a nice person." Curly wasn't satisfied with that, so he went on. "I think I'm falling for her. I'm thinking about telling her I love her and that I want her to marry me. What do you think about that?"

Mr. Levine again thought for a while. Those lines I'd seen so many times appeared on his forehead. I knew he was thinking about what he was going to say to Curly, just like I always knew when he was going to say something to me. After a couple of minutes he took Curly's hand in both of his hands. He looked straight at him and said, "Curly, you're a good man. Annemaria's a good woman. I knew her mother. Her memory is a blessing. You could do a lot worse." Curly visibly relaxed when he heard those words, but I knew there was going to be more. I just knew.

"Curly," Mr. Levine said, "How long have you been seeing her?" Curly answered, "About a month." Mr. Levine, still holding onto Curly's hand said, very quietly, "I think you might be right for each other, but are you very sure you love her after just a month? Do you think she could love you after just a month? Let me tell you something, you better be sure about that." And Curly said, "I think I'm sure David. I think I'm sure."

"Let me tell you something else," Mr. Levine said. "If you love her, okay. If you only think you love her, that's another story. Listen to me, and never forget what I'm telling you," he said. "Never say I love you unless you know what you're talking about."

Curly smiled sheepishly and said, "You're right, David, you're right. Maybe we need a little more time." Mr. Levine finally released Curly's hand and Curly thanked him, gave him a hug, waved at me, and left.

I wished I'd remembered about Curly on the New Year's Eve when I told Victoria I thought I loved her. And I was so very glad Mr. Levine had not said, "Curly, I'm gonna tell you something and I

Never Say I Love You Unless You Know What You're Talking About

want you should remember it for the rest of your life." Those words belong to me.

If You Succeed at Something, Try Something Harder

It was the 1952-53 school year. I was twelve years old and in the seventh grade. My previous two years of school had been spent learning with just one teacher, Miss Maskel. I remember her as the best schoolteacher I ever knew. She was very important in my young life, just like Mr. Levine.

Moving on to junior high was a big deal to me. It was different than elementary school. I had five classroom teachers, one each for English, Math, Science, History, and Social Studies, instead of just one. At first it was a little strange to have to go from room to room carrying all my books. Actually, it was a little confusing. All the seventh graders were always looking at their class schedules for the first week or so to be sure they would end up at the right classroom. A bell ended each class period and you had to get to your next class before the bell rang again five minutes later. There was no recess like there had been in elementary school.

Instead there was Gym. I never liked gym class. The teacher acted as if everyone had to be in love with sports. Kids like me were okay with a pickup game with friends, but being assigned a position for baseball and having to learn the rules for volleyball or some other sport held zero interest for me. I sometimes tried to cut

If You Succeed at Something, Try Something Harder

that class, but I usually got caught and would have to run three or four laps around the schoolyard as punishment.

My first semester ended with a not-so-great report card. I got four Cs and a D in my academic classes, and a 'Satisfactory' in Gym. The note on the report card from my homeroom teacher said I was "not reaching my potential." My mother was not too happy with it. "How do you expect to get into college?" she asked me more than once. I didn't care about getting into college then. That was for my sister and maybe my brother. So I listened and said nothing in response. I was thinking that it was better to get a job than to go to college. The next semester, though, I must have gotten the message, because when report cards came out I had straight As, and my Satisfactory in Gym had moved up to a Good. There was no note from the homeroom teacher this time. My mother was thrilled and bragged to her friends that Michael, her baby, got straight A's on his report card. I hated it when she did that. I was the youngest, but not a baby. Even so, I sometimes bragged about it myself.

School was over for the year right after I got that straight-A report card. It was about a week later, after sweeping the bakery on a Sunday afternoon, that Mr. Levine asked me about school. He'd come back to work a week or so after he got out of the hospital following his heart attack back in May, just before my birthday. "How did you do in school?" he asked. I puffed up a little and said, "I got straight As." And he asked me if that had been hard to do. I told him it was. I had to read a lot of books and write about the American Revolution for History, the way Congress works for Social Studies, take a lot of tests in Math and Science, and write a short story for my English class. "So, how hard was it?" Mr. Levine asked. I told him it was real hard, but I got straight As.

Mr. Levine looked at me with that look I had come to know. He was about to tell me something that he wanted me to remember for the rest of my life. Sure enough, he did. He congratulated me on getting straight As. He praised me for doing something that I thought was hard. He reminded me three or four times about how successful

Mr. Levine and Me

I was, and then finally he came to the point and said, "Michael, I'm gonna tell you something and I want you should remember it for the rest of your life. If you succeed at something, try something harder."

That was the end of the conversation. Mr. Levine went behind the counter, waved at me and said, "See you tomorrow."

Walking home from the bakery I wondered about what Mr. Levine had told me. I didn't really do anything about it then, and not for years afterward. But I remember those words of his. I also remember that as I made my way through life, once I got past, as I think of it, my "trouble time," I was always looking for something harder to do. It was never enough to succeed at something. There was always a new challenge around the corner. If something was good, I wanted to make it better. That idea ultimately extended to every part of life for me. There is always something harder. If you try it, you may succeed. If you don't you can try it again, but if you do, it's best to find something even harder. Thanks for that, Mr. Levine.

Today, I Am a Man

When I was eleven and still sweeping out the bakery every afternoon, my stepfather Morris' father died. Morris was not a religious person in the traditional sense, but when his father died, he decided that he was going to follow the Jewish custom of reciting the mourner's prayer, or Kaddish, every day for a year at synagogue with a community of worshippers. The synagogue we attended at that time was Temple Keser Israel on Sherman Avenue, not too far from where we were living then. A daily service was held there each weekday morning and Sundays at seven a.m., attended mostly by a few old guys who had nothing else to do. And, of course, there were regular sabbath services on Friday evenings and Saturday mornings. Each day, Morris walked from our apartment to the synagogue, attended the brief morning service during which he recited the mourner's prayer, and then crossed over Chapel Street where he caught the downtown bus in front of St. Raphael's hospital. After a time I started going to the synagogue with him. I did it almost every day. I'm not sure why I decided to do it, but after a time I got used to going there with Morris every morning and it became part of my regular routine.

There were a couple of bonuses in it for me. The first of these was that the dozen or so old men who attended these weekday services loved the idea that there was a kid present. That was really unusual. Kids never came on weekday mornings. After the service Morris would leave immediately because he had to get downtown to work, but I had time to hang around for a while because it would be at least forty-five minutes before school began for me, and my school

Mr. Levine and Me

was only a few blocks away. They always served danish pastries and coffee following the service, and I took advantage of that. The old men would have a snort of schnapps with their coffee, and I'd have a glass of milk and a danish. Sometimes one of the old guys would give me a quarter, just because.

The other bonus, something that would come in handy later on, was that I was learning all the Hebrew texts of the service by rote, just by being there each day. After a time I was chanting the service right along with Morris and the old guys. I didn't even realize fully that it was happening. I also didn't realize that the things I was learning were the very same things I'd need to master when I began my instructions for my Bar Mitzvah with the cantor and rabbi a little later that year.

A couple of months down the road I began to meet with the cantor, Morris Silverman, for a weekly bar mitzvah lesson. He was a man with a magnificent tenor voice who led the services at the synagogue, accompanied by a mixed choir and pipe organ. His job was to get me to learn how to conduct a sabbath morning service, and he was surprised that I already knew just about the entire service, which made his job easier. He also had to teach me to chant a passage from the Torah, as well as a selection from one of the Prophets. All of it in Hebrew, of course. At the time I thought it was a pretty strange exercise since, although I learned how to read the Hebrew, I had virtually no comprehension of the meaning of what I was reading. I knew even then that it was the ritual that was important, rather than the message. That didn't make a lot of sense to me, but it was just the way it was. As the time neared for my Bar Mitzvah I worked with Rabbi Klein, who helped me write my speech, a little discourse on the meaning of the Torah reading. After a while I mastered everything I needed to know for a credible bar mitzvah, and on May 14, 1954, the ceremony took place.

I led the community in the beginning parts of the service as people were still arriving. The sanctuary slowly filled with people, some of them the regulars I recognized from when I had attended

Today, I Am a Man

with my stepfather as he memorialized his father. I saw my friends Bobby, Joey, and Ash Wednesday when they arrived. They came even though the teaching of their church at the time was opposed to Catholics going to houses of worship that were not Catholic. My mother and Morris were seated near the front of the sanctuary along with my brother, my sister, and my grandparents, uncles, aunts, and cousins. Some of my mother's friends were there too, seated in the rows behind her. I remember Blondie with her bright red lipstick and bleached close-cut hair especially as she looked up at me, a big smile on her face the entire time.

When it came time for the part of the service when the Torah scroll was paraded around the sanctuary, with the Cantor and choir singing a march tempo hymn and me carrying the heavy Torah scroll, I was the center of attention. Each person along the aisles reached out to touch the scroll with a prayer book or the with the fringes of a prayer shawl. Just about every one of them said some complimentary thing to me. It felt good, all of it. And then, in a complete surprise, as I reached the rear of the sanctuary carrying that Torah scroll, there he was: Mr. Levine. He reached out and touched the scroll with his prayer book, then kissed the spine of the book. He smiled and did something no one else had done. He wrapped his arms around my shoulders, drew me in, Torah scroll and all, for a hug. He kissed me on the cheek and softly said, "Mazel tov, Michael, mazel tov." Then I completed my march around the sanctuary, ascended the pulpit, and finished up what I was supposed to finish up.

After the service, everyone went to the social hall for a reception my mother and her friends had put together. Bagels, lox and cream cheese, pickled herring in wine sauce, cookies and cakes, coffee, tea, schnapps, and other things were there for everyone. Every adult congratulated me, and some of them handed me envelopes with gifts in them. Mr. Levine was not among them. I guess he left when the service concluded. In my mind the most important thing about that Saturday morning was not anything I had accomplished, not the

Mr. Levine and Me

obvious pride and pleasure on the faces of my mother and Morris, not seeing my friends Bobby, Joey, and Ash Wednesday defying the rules of their church to be with me, not all the words of congratulations from people I knew and from people I didn't know. None of that. The most important thing to me was that Mr. Levine had been there.

The following day I didn't go with Morris and Uncle Harry to get the things for Sunday brunch. I think they went to Westville that day and not to our old neighborhood. Instead I rode my bicycle over to Legion Avenue. It took more than half an hour to get there. I walked into the bakery with my bike like I owned the place and asked the woman behind the counter if Mr. Levine was around. She waved at the door to the bakery and, without asking, I went in. Mr. Levine was busy at the work bench making those knotted rolls he once taught me how to make. No one else was there, but he didn't hear me come in. I watched him for a couple minutes as he very quickly formed the rolls and placed them on the pan. He was like an artist, placing each of the rolls in precisely the right spot on the tray.

Finally I stopped watching him and went to the corner of the bakery where the broom, my old broom, was kept. I began sweeping. It felt good to be doing that again. After a minute or two I let the broom bump into something and the sound broke Mr. Levine's concentration. He turned and saw me, and the best smile I had ever seen on him filled the bakery with light. I leaned the broom against the big mixer and ran across the bakery to Mr. Levine. He looked at me, still smiling.

We stood there talking for a few minutes about the bar mitzvah service, about how he was feeling, about how school was going for me as eighth grade was coming to an end, about this and that.

After a while Mr. Levine's smile faded and he looked me in the eyes. "Michael," he said. "Do you know what yesterday means? What your Bar Mitzvah means?" He didn't wait for me to answer. "It means that now you are responsible for whatever you do for the rest of your life. The blessing Morris said after you finished reading

Today, I Am a Man

Torah means, 'Praised is God, who has relieved me of responsibility for him,' meaning you. The way it works is that your parents are responsible for your mistakes when you are a child, but when you do a bar mitzvah you become in some magic way responsible for yourself. Michael, try to remember that. That's the way it really is." We talked for a while longer, catching up, just like grownups do. And then it was time for me to head home. Mr. Levine walked me to the door and waved goodbye as I took off on my bike.

Riding back home along Sherman Avenue I told myself I was no longer a child. "Today, I am a man." I said it aloud.

Ochi Chernye: Dark Eyes

I always liked going to my grandmother Sophie's. She made the best food. Pierogis filled with potatoes and onion, and kasha knishes, holubtsi, kielbasa kapusta, and my favorite of all soups, what my grandmother called "depression soup." She called it that because during the Great Depression everybody could come up with an onion and a few potatoes and a little salt and pepper. I make that very soup once in a while to this day, and when I do I feel the presence of Bubbe Sofia. That she is present in an old photo hanging in my kitchen probably helps bring that feeling on.

She had a silver music box candy dish that was always filled with those oblong hard filled candies, wrapped in wax paper printed with a picture of whatever fruit flavor was inside the hard shell of the candy. We couldn't just go to the candy dish, though. My grandmother had a collection of little figurines that lived on the wide sill of the bay window in the living room. She kept them in a particular order and when any of us kids were around she'd ask us to guess which of the figurines was missing. We'd study the collection long and hard, trying to remember all of the figurines and then trying to figure out which one was missing. If one of us guessed correctly, that person could go first to the candy dish. Of course the rest of us followed close behind. If no one guessed right, we still got to go to the candy dish and help ourselves. I remember that when the cover of the candy dish was lifted it began to play the song "Smoke Gets in Your Eyes," in tinkling music box style.

Another thing I liked about Grandma's home was the big Victrola in the corner of the living room. It had to be cranked before a record

Ochi Chernye: Dark Eyes

could be played on it. She had a big pile of record albums. They were different from what we think of today as record albums. There were no CDs, of course, and records in those days would shatter if you dropped them on the floor. My grandmother had records from Europe that were big, thick black discs, recorded on just one side. They were kept in big albums that looked like fat notebooks stuffed with heavy brown envelopes that held each record. When we were there visiting, she would always let one of the kids crank the Victrola, and she would play some of her favorites. They weren't big band, doo wop, or jazz. They were mostly classical. Opera, symphonies, and the like. If she wasn't playing records, the radio was on.

Once while I was there the announcer on the radio said that if anyone had an original recording of the Great Caruso and got it to the station within an hour, that person would win 15,000 S&H green stamps that could be redeemed for merchandise at the S&H store. My grandmother got more excited than I had ever seen her before. She had an original recording of Caruso. She got it from her stack of albums, along with its heavy envelope, put it into a shopping bag and told me to take it on my bike to the radio station. "Be careful," she said. "Don't break it." I made it to the radio station downtown, and my grandmother won the books of S&H green stamps. While I was at the radio station the record was played on the air after the announcer mentioned that it was an original, recorded on just one side, from Deutsche Grammophon and that it had been sent by Mrs. Sophie Ewanuff. When I got back to Grandma's, everyone was excited when I handed over the shopping bag that now had not only the record, but also many, many books of green stamps.

Grandma put on another record, not Caruso but another singer. The song was "Ochi Chernye," ("Black Eyes"). I'd heard that song many times before, both at my grandparents' house and also when my mother sang it once in a while. A few years later I learned it was not only my grandmother's favorite song, but Mr. Levine's also. I still remember the melody and a few of the Russian words, even now. I never learned the full translation when I was a child but here it is (I looked it up on Wikipedia):

Ochi Chernye
Black eyes, passionate eyes,
Burning and beautiful eyes!
How I love you, how I revere you,
It seems I met you in an unlucky hour!

Oh, not for nothing are you darker than the deep!
I see mourning for my soul in you,
I see a triumphant flame in you:
A poor heart burning in it.

But I am not sad, I am not sorrowful,
My fate is soothing to me:
All that is best in life that God gave us,
In sacrifice I returned to the fiery eyes.

One of the last times I was with Mr. Levine was in 1958, just before I went into the Army. I had quit school when I was sixteen and had been mostly just hanging around doing not much of anything. I hardly ever went to Legion Avenue anymore. Things were so different there. It had gone from run down to really run down as the slummy area around Oak Street, which was really the other end of Legion Avenue, crept closer and closer. Some of the stores had closed and it would be just a few years before all of them would be gone forever. Mr. Levine was not at the bakery every day either. After his heart attack he had slowed down. He was seventy-five years old when that had happened, four years before.

I rode my bicycle from where I lived with Morris and my mother on Norton Parkway to the bakery. I still had the Raleigh English three-speed, skinny-tired bike, once beautiful and the best bike on the avenue, which I had won for selling one hundred and

Ochi Chernye: Dark Eyes

eighty-eight Boy Scout Jamboree tickets, with a little help from Mr. Levine. I'd long ago removed the fenders and chain cover guard to make it lighter. Some of the coating on the brake cables was cracked, and there were scratches and a few dents on it. Only the front brakes worked. It wasn't so beautiful anymore, but it still got me around. I had a car by that time, a 1941 Oldsmobile that an old lady I had cut grass for over several summers had given me, just because she wanted to. I think maybe it had something to do with the fact that I never charged her for cutting her grass. She was a widow, and as poor as everyone around the neighborhood. I think I cut her grass for free because Mr. Levine's words, "If somebody needs your help, help them," kicked in and inspired me to do it. You might be wondering why I rode my bicycle to the bakery instead of driving the car. I didn't have any gas money and the car was sitting on empty. The story of my life, I guess.

When I got to the bakery I chained my bike to a street sign. You had to do that around Legion Avenue in that time or it would be stolen for sure. I saw Mr. Levine through the window and I was so glad he was there. I went in, and he came out from behind the counter. He had seen me when I was putting the lock on my bike and now, just like old times, he brought a plate with a couple of cookies on it out to the table by the window. He put the plate down and I reached out to shake his hand, but he hugged me instead. "Michael, you look like a man. Do you want coffee?" I nodded, and he poured a cup for each of us. We sat down together and I told him I'd be leaving for basic training at Fort Dix, New Jersey, in a week.

"So, you're gonna be a soldier?" he asked. I told him all about enlisting with my high school friend, George Washington Carver James, and he smiled, not saying anything. He asked me what I'd been doing with myself. He had heard that I wasn't going to school. I told him I wasn't doing much of anything. He also asked me what made me decide to join the Army, and I told him that my sister's father-in-law had suggested it, because he thought it would help me get my life on track.

Mr. Levine and Me

We talked like that for a while, back and forth, about this and that. And then Mr. Levine got up and went back behind the counter. "I want you should hear something, Michael," he said. He had a record in his hand and he put it on a record player that was behind the counter. I never knew there was a record player in the bakery, and I was a little surprised to see it. Mr. Levine carefully put the record on the turntable, started it, and gently placed the arm with its needle down on the record. After a few moments of scratchiness a violin began to play. It sounded familiar to me, and I wondered why. Then a man with a baritone voice began to sing and I remembered. It was "Ochi Chernye," one of my grandmother's favorites that I had heard so many times at her home after I cranked the Victrola. I laid my head down on my hands and listened. I wondered if there was some reason Mr. Levine was playing this record then. He always had a reason for everything.

After a few minutes, the music stopped and the scratchy sound came back. Mr. Levine got up and gently lifted the needle from the record, then put the record back into its cover.

"Do you like that song, Michael?" he asked. I told him I had heard that song lots of times at my grandmother's house. It was her favorite song, I told him. "You know, Michael," he said, "it's my favorite song too, and was my Kateryna's also. Every time I listen to it I see her beautiful black eyes and her smile. She's with me when I hear it, just like before."

Mr. Levine had told me, when he was in the hospital after his heart attack, about his wife, Kateryna, and how much he loved her. He'd only been married to her for five and a half years, but he loved her then and through all the many years since. And "Ochi Chernye" had the magical power to bring her back to him.

"When my Kateryna died, her memory is for blessing," he said, "I had a friend at the Ukrainian Orthodox Church. He used to lead the services there, just like a cantor in the synagogue does. He had a beautiful voice. I asked him if he would sing 'Ochi Chernye' for me and for Kateryna at her funeral. He said he would if it was all

Ochi Chernye: Dark Eyes

right with the rabbi. It was okay with the rabbi, and what I remember most about that day was 'Ochi Chernye,' her favorite song. I never needed to remember the eulogy. Her eulogy was, and it still is, in my heart."

I was seventeen years old, just about to go into the Army, and there I was, crying like a little boy as I listened to Mr. Levine that day.

I spent time with Mr. Levine just one more time after that day. It was in 1959, when Morris died. Mr. Levine seemed much older then. His face was more deeply lined. He was a little stooped over. He walked slowly. He was very thin. He was still Mr. Levine, but not the Mr. Levine who had something to tell me about everything. I hadn't heard his almost magical incantation: "Michael, I'm gonna tell you something and I want you should remember it for the rest of your life," for several years by the time I learned about his favorite song and what it meant to him.

Mr. Levine died in 1961. I didn't know until much later. But when I did know I heard the strains of "Ochi Chernye," not in the voice of some great baritone, but in the raspy, Yiddish accented voice of Mr. Levine. He was singing, in my mind, to his beloved Kateryna.

Learn to Bake Bread

Mr. Levine once told me he made a pretty good living running a bakery. It was hard work making all that bread dough and forming loaves or rolls or bagels. It wasn't easy starting days at four in the morning so fresh bread would be ready for customers at seven. Bags of flour were heavy and had to be moved from one place to another all the time. But it was all worth it. The day Mr. Levine told me about the good life of a baker, he spoke almost lovingly about the process of turning flour and yeast and water into bread. He smiled a lot as he spoke, and his hands moved as if he were kneading dough in a bowl or on the work table out back. I think he really loved that he was a baker. This was true even though he sometimes complained that his back always hurt from lugging sacks of flour around.

Mr. Levine told me that he wondered how people first figured out how to make bread. There are a lot of steps in the process that we take for granted. In the beginning there were no flour mills, no yeast. Salt was an expensive commodity, and you couldn't go to a store and buy a bag of sugar. And also, before people began to make bread thousands of years ago, no one even knew you could do it.

I'd never heard Mr. Levine talk like this before. He went on for quite a while about what he thought must have been the beginning of bread making. He said it must have been an accident, or maybe a miracle. Maybe, he speculated, people were eating wild grains like the animals and birds did. Early people just ate whatever they could find, and somehow they knew that if the birds and animals could eat something, then they could probably eat it too. And then, he said, once people learned how to make fire, another accident probably

Learn to Bake Bread

born of a lightning strike, they also learned how to keep it going, and because of that, cooking was born. Maybe some mother figured out that it would be easier for little children to eat the wild grains they gathered if they cooked them for a while in water to soften them up. That, of course, required making something that could hold water and withstand the heat of a fire. But that's a different story about pottery.

Mr. Levine went on talking about how maybe some cooked grains didn't get eaten and then were left in a ceramic pot for a few days, until that unknown and unsung mother noticed that the cooked grains had become bubbly. Wild yeasts were busy at work. At some point someone had the idea of grinding grains between two stones into a coarse powder and adding it to some bubbly old, for lack of a better name, porridge, until it was thick enough to pick up. And someone else thought it would be a good idea to stick a hunk of it to the outside of a ceramic pot sitting on the fire. And like that, Mr. Levine said happily, the first bread was made.

It wasn't like modern bread, but if you could get it unstuck it was edible. Over time, making crude bread in the same place over and over again resulted in a yeasty environment. And that was, magically, the birth of sourdough. From there it was only a matter of time before some primitive human, maybe a child playing with the dough ball as if it were a toy, squeezing it and throwing it around, accidentally came up with the idea of kneading. Because of that, finer breads came into being and laid the foundation for all the many centuries of bread baking that followed. By the time a couple of millennia had gone by, bread became known as the staff of life.

Mr. Levine went on and on about bread that day. I wasn't a bread baker. I didn't think I would ever be a bread baker, at least not one who baked bread for a living. I liked hearing all about it, though, from Mr. Levine. I don't know that he was correct about any of it, but that doesn't matter. After a while he stopped talking about bread. He smiled and looked at me. Then he said, "Michael, you should learn to bake bread. If you do, you'll never go hungry. Flour is cheap."

Many years later I started baking my own bread. It was slow going at first. Sometimes it turned out okay. Other times not so much. But after a while the results got better and my rye breads, challahs, whole wheat, Italian and French breads often filled my kitchen with that special aroma that only comes from bread baking in the oven. It still does. I often share fresh-baked breads with friends, and it brings a smile to their faces every time. And (I think Mr. Levine would like this), I haven't bought a loaf of bread from a store in more than thirty years. I bake bread every week. And yes, flour is cheap.

Dmitro, I'm Gonna Tell You Something

Mr. Levine was eighty-one years old the last time I visited with him. I was still in the Army, home on leave for the funeral of my stepfather Morris. He still worked at the bakery, although he told me he was done lugging those big bags of flour around. He was visibly older than the last time I saw him less than a year before. He worked only in the front of the bakery by that time, and not every day like before. The heaviest thing he had to lift was a bag with a few bagels or rolls in it. He didn't want to stop working in the back, but he was no longer able to do the work he really loved, baking bread. That was for someone else to do. I don't think he was really sad about that, but I think he would have liked it if he were still able to do it. Of course he accepted the reality of his situation. I wonder if he spoke quietly to himself as he had spoken to me all those many times. "I'm gonna tell you something and I want you should remember it for the rest of your life: Never do more than you can do." I think that's pretty good Levine-ism. Maybe I have a future as a wannabe Mr. Levine.

I spent a few hours with Mr. Levine that Sunday in 1959. We talked about some of the things we had talked about years before. We laughed about the time he caught me in a lie and about when I won my bicycle. We remembered so many of the things we talked about when I was the sweeper of the bakery. He wondered what was going on with my friends Bobby, Joey, and Ash Wednesday. Neither

Mr. Levine and Me

of us knew. They had left the neighborhood not long after I did. We both cried a little when we remembered my visits to the hospital after his heart attack. And at the end of our talking that day, as I was about to leave, he stood up and hugged me. It was only the second time he had ever done that. The first was on the day of my Bar Mitzvah, more than five years before. That hug and this one were for me, then and now, the best hugs I've ever gotten from anyone.

When I left the bakery that day and stepped out into the changed landscape of Legion Avenue, I knew there would never again be a place like that place had been. There would never be another Mr. Levine at a bakery ready to guide some other kid along whatever pathway he was on. I felt a sense of joy that there had been a Legion Avenue for me, and a Mr. Levine for me. I'm still glad about those things today. They are still real for me, alive in whatever the magic is that we call memory.

I thought about Mr. Levine as I went back to my mother's apartment. A couple of her old friends were there when I arrived. It was still the week for shiva visits. Her best old friend Ruth (or Blondie, as we knew her) gave me a hug and said, "I'm glad you're back. Go make some coffee—only you can make a good cup of coffee." When I was very young, Blondie always asked me to make the coffee if we were visiting at her house. Like the little kid I used to be, I obeyed her once again and started a new pot. After a while, once my mother's friends left, I helped get everything cleaned up. I was going to be leaving the next morning to return to Fort Sill. I felt like I had come to the end of an era.

The next morning I took the train to New York and got myself to LaGuardia for my flight to Oklahoma. My unit had shipped out to Germany while I was on leave, so I wouldn't be back with George Washington Carver James or any of the other friends I'd made in the Army. I served just a few more months until I was offered an early out, and I took it. I think that moment, the moment I was discharged from the Army, was the end of my childhood. I was not yet nineteen years old. Life had barely begun. I was about to enter a new phase,

Dmitro, I'm Gonna Tell You Something

and Legion Avenue and Mr. Levine wouldn't be a part of it. I never lived in New Haven again. I never saw Mr. Levine again. That part of living was over, and I knew there would never be a replacement.

Dmitro Levyitskyi, Mr. Levine, I'm gonna tell you something and I want you should remember it forever and ever: There'll never be another like you. Stay with me always.

And you know, he has.

Mr. Levine died in 1961. He was eighty-three years old. His memory is for blessing.

Epilogue

All the stories related in this book are true, at least as I remember them. The timeline may be a little off here and there, and some of the details a little fuzzy. Memory, as we all know, is not perfect. The stories are not chronologically ordered but randomly placed because that's the way I think memory works. The past is recalled, at least for me, as one singular moment. Everything is mixed up together like a ball of yarn from which we can pull a string from here and from there. Although I'm now in my eighties, my memories from childhood don't seem to be distant memories, but rather seem as if they are happening in the moment as they open in my mind.

Some of the sayings of Mr. Levine in this book may be from more than one person I knew when I was a child. I was lucky enough to have known several people with what Yiddish calls לעכס (*seichel*), meaning common sense, reason, intelligence, smarts, etc., who gave me lessons for living. Each of them contributed parts of whatever wisdom I may have acquired over the years. So some of the sayings I've attributed to Mr. Levine may be, in actuality, from more than one wise person. I can't remember for sure.

I remember some of the many Ukrainian immigrants who visited my grandparents' home to share a pot of Sweet Touch Nee tea and have conversations about the old country. Many of them had changed their names, just like Mr. Levine. My grandfather, Michael Ewanuff, never changed his name, but both of my uncles did. Uncle Henry substituted Wayne for Ewanuff, and Uncle Harry became Harry Evans. I remember my grandfather sometimes saying, "Everybody, stand up: It's the illustrious Mr. Evans," if Uncle Harry

Epilogue

entered the room. What I'm getting at here is that it was commonplace for immigrants or members of their families to do that so they could better fit in. Mr. Levine did it too when Dmitro Levyitskyi became David Levine.

Mr. Levine is still a very real person for me. He lives on in memory and still, sometimes, informs me about how I might think as I approach some circumstance or other. "Michael," he so often said, "I'm gonna tell you something and I want you should remember it for the rest of your life."

I have. I hear him complimenting me for that right now as I type the last words of this book.

Thanks for everything, Mr. Levine. You're the best.

PART 2

THIRTY-MINUTE FRIENDS

People I Meet Again Along the Pathways of My Mind

Prologue

When I think of people I encounter who I may never see again but who have impacted me in some meaningful way, many memories come to mind. Here is one:

Once when I was riding on the subway from Times Square back to Queens, the train stopped along the way and a bunch of school kids in their young teens got on board. They were a little rowdy, as kids that age can often be. One of the boys cursed at one of the other boys. The boy doing the cursing was tall and fit looking. Near where he was standing an elderly woman was sitting. She was tiny, with graying hair, wearing glasses, looking kind of frail.

The woman stood up and went over to the boy who had sworn at the other boy, looked up at him towering over her and said, "Does your mama know you talk like that out in public? You sit yourself down and shut your mouth!" Everyone on that subway car went silent. The boy hung his head down and said, "Yes Ma'am," and found himself a seat.

The woman went back to her seat. A few people gave her a round of applause. I never spoke to her. I knew I would never see her again. But I also knew I would see her again, somewhere along the pathways in my mind, the same ones I've explored as I was writing this book. I count her as among my thirty-minute friends.

As we go through our lives we encounter many people. We see them but we don't know them. It's as if they are random images on a screen, there for a moment and then gone forever.

Prologue

There is a truth we don't usually think about, and it's that each of the people we pass on the street has a story. The clerk at the checkout counter in the grocery store has a story. So does the person who changes the oil in our cars, and the hamburger flipper at the fast-food place, and the librarian, the plumber, the waiter and busboy at our favorite restaurant, the bus driver, and the barista. Even members of our own families have stories. Each of the people we see every day of our lives has a story that is important to someone, at the least to themselves. And maybe the stories they carry around with them would be important to us if we knew what they were.

Over the years I've had interactions with people that I know I will never see again. Those kinds of meetings can last for a few moments or an hour, or even a few months or sometimes years. Some of these have been with people in my family as well. Each of them has been a unique experience. Informative in some way, even important. And the fact that those moments of connection occurred between people who we might never meet again does not negate their importance. Each and every experience is important. We usually don't realize this in the moment, but sometimes upon reflection, maybe even after years have passed, we come to realize there is treasure in the memories of chance encounters, or in events that may seem banal in the moment. Important encounters don't need to include two-way communication. Sometimes a few words or some simple actions are enough to create a memory that has great value, a memory to be called upon at some future time that will help to illuminate the path that is always before each of us.

The moments I revisit in the pages of this book are memories from pieces of my life. There is something funny about the way memories arise. It's never an orderly list of things that happened. I think of one incident and it somehow calls to mind many others. It's not a chronological outline of things that happened. Rather it's a random collection of thoughts living on the ends of their incomprehensible neurons, each of them just waiting to pop up unexpectedly because of some seemingly unrelated other thought. I don't know how it works. I think nobody knows how it works. But it does. Every moment of every life has its own unique place in the saga of that life, and I think there is some unknown and unknowable mechanism that brings each of them to life when the time is ripe.

I think of some of these moments as memories of thirty-minute friends. Even though I may not see the people I remember this way again, I think of them as part of my circle of friends. Moments I share with long-term acquaintances or friends or family often have great importance embedded within them. But sometimes a memory of a brief moment in time, witnessing or hearing something, meeting someone for a brief time, exchanging but a few words, may be stronger than what we often think of as kinship or friendship. I think that is because most people we identify as friends, acquaintances or colleagues, and the fact that we may be with them for long stretches of time does not make the memory of them more important than the memory of a connection that lasted but a moment or a few minutes.

I've enjoyed exploring these moments along the path of my life. I've learned some things about myself and the meanings behind some of the twists and turns of that never-ending path. I hope that when I reread the things I've written on these pages, other memories will arise. If that happens my life will be further enriched.

So, with all that being said, what you will read in the following pages are accounts of moments that I think of as encounters with thirty-minute friends. I hope that as you read some of the vignettes you'll find on the pages beyond this one, you will be inspired to think of other such moments and people you've experienced and met along the way from your own deep reservoir of thought and memory, and be moved and inspired by those memories.

A Confession

When I was about eleven or twelve years old, I was friends with Bobby and Joey, and we were all friends with another kid we always called Ash Wednesday because of the prominent mole in the middle of his forehead. We played together, hung around together, ate in each other's homes, listened and obeyed with equal attention any of our parents, and acted more like family than as neighbors or friends.

On school days our time together was pretty limited, but on Saturdays we often spent the whole day together doing this or that and somehow managing to stay out of trouble. After dinner we were allowed to get out of our houses until nine or even ten o'clock. Almost every Saturday after dinner I would meet up with Bobby and Joey and we'd go to Ash Wednesday's back yard. He lived with his parents on the second floor of a three-family house. Bobby, Joey, and I would call out, "Hey, Ash Wednesday...." and invariably his mother would appear on the second-floor porch and loudly say the same words in her immigrant Italian accent, "You no calla my son Ash-a Wednesday." Ash Wednesday would come down to the back yard and as we started to leave his mother would shout, "Don't go nowhere until you go to confession!"

Bobby, Joey, and Ash Wednesday were all Catholics, and they knew they had to go to confession every week. As we walked to the church each Saturday, the three of them would try to talk me into going to confession with them. Of course they knew I was Jewish and that going to confession wasn't part of my religion, but they persisted. Sometimes I said to them, "That's a Catholic thing. Leave me alone." But they finally convinced me and I agreed to do it. They taught me as we walked toward the church what I was supposed to say once I was seated in the confessional booth, and I thought I was ready.

When we got to the church we all went in and got in line behind a lot of other people, adults and kids, and waited our turn. I remember feeling very nervous and maybe a little bit afraid about what I was doing, but I couldn't back out. Bobby, Joey, and Ash Wednesday took their turns going into the confessional booths as they emptied. Then I was next in the line, and when someone left one of the booths I went in to take their place.

For someone who hadn't grown up with this practice it was all kind of spooky. The confessionals were in a dimly lit area at the back of the church. Nobody in the line of would-be confessors was talking. The hush was palpable. Once inside the booth it was even spookier to me. As I closed the door behind me, I noticed that the opening in the wall of the confessional was covered with a metal screen with little holes in it. A curtain swished open on the opposite side of the screen, and I could see the outline of someone on the other side. I knew it was one of the priests because my friends had told me how things would be. So I recited what Bobby, Joey, and Ash Wednesday had taught me: "Bless me Father, for I have sinned. My last confession was three weeks ago." I stopped speaking because that was all Bobby, Joey, and Ash Wednesday had told me to say. I remained silent for quite a while until finally a voice from the other side of the screen said, "Well?" and I responded, "Well what?" Then the voice said, "You've come here to confess your sins. What is it you would like to confess?" I thought about that for a few seconds, getting more and more nervous about this thing I was doing, and I answered, "I don't know." And the voice behind the screen said, "Was it a venial sin or a mortal sin?"

I thought about it for a minute. I had never heard the words "venial sin" or "mortal sin" before, and I blurted out, "I don't know. I'm Jewish!" Then I opened the door and ran out of there. My friends thought the whole thing was hilarious and they were laughing and

A Confession

punching me in the arm to express their approval of what I had done. Then we went on to our usual Saturday night of hanging out.

For the next few days I worried about my experience with confession. I had a feeling that I had done something really bad, almost as if I had been insulting, or making fun of, an important part of the lives of most of the people who lived in my neighborhood. I even wondered if God was unhappy with me. One day though, it all got cleared up for me. Walking down the street one afternoon with Bobby, Joey, and Ash Wednesday, we saw three nuns and a young priest coming toward us. They were carrying grocery bags back from Legion Avenue to the Rectory. As we neared each other the priest said to me with a smile on his face, "Hey Michael, been to confession lately?"

I wondered how the priest knew what I had done. I figured he was able to see me through the screen of the confessional, even though I was unable to see him. Or maybe Bobby, Joey, or Ash Wednesday had told him what they had done to get me to go to confession the next time they went back themselves. It was not strange to me that the priest knew my name, because all the kids in the neighborhood, Catholic or not, were in the church pretty often playing basketball or ping pong in the recreation space in the church basement. That simple remark by a kindly young Catholic priest made a Jewish kid feel better about the terrible thing he thought he had done.

There's one more little piece of this story. About a year after making my first and only Catholic confession, it was time for me to celebrate my Bar Mitzvah. Back then, the Church's official teaching was that Catholics could not worship anywhere but in a Catholic church. My friends Bobby, Joey, and Ash Wednesday went to that very same priest and told him they wanted to attend my Bar Mitzvah ceremony at the synagogue. They told him I had come to their confirmation ceremonies and they really wanted to be there for my special day. The priest told them that church teaching did not allow for this, but then added, "If you happen to go to Michael's synagogue for his Bar Mitzvah, come to confession that evening and make sure you get me."

Every time I think of this episode I'm appreciative of the kindness and understanding of that priest.

The Aboriginal Man

Once, when I was visiting Sydney, Australia, I met one of my thirty-minute friends. I was walking around the harbor area. The magnificent Sydney Opera House was, of course, one of the places every tourist wanted to see. I spent quite a bit of time admiring the beauty of that building, which looked like a sailing ship at the edge of the water. After that I continued my walk and it became a bit uncomfortable because of the multitude of tiny sand flies that seemed to be everywhere. Everyone was waving their hands in front of their faces to shoo them away, and I was doing the same. It became almost intolerable and so, when I noticed an art museum, I decided to go in to look at the art and get away from the ubiquitous flies.

As I entered the museum I noticed an Aboriginal man sitting on one of the viewing benches. He was very still as he sat crosslegged on the bench. His gaze was directed to the painting on the wall before him. He was so still that he seemed to be statuary, part of the exhibit, rather than a person viewing a work of art. I watched him for five or ten minutes. He never moved. He seemed not to be breathing. I wondered what was going through his mind as he sat there so still and silent. He looked serene, black as onyx, a mass of curls topping his head, wrinkles on his face. I think he was tall, but he could have been short. It was hard to know because of the way he was sitting.

After a while I began to wander through the museum. I stopped here and there to take a closer look at a painting. I sat on one or another of the viewing benches from time to time and enjoyed whichever painting I was viewing. It was a nice, quiet, and peaceful interlude. I spent more than three hours wandering that museum until finally I decided it was time for me to get out among the sand flies and people, tourists like me, and enjoy a little more of Sydney. When I got to the exit, the same door I had entered some four hours before, I saw the Aboriginal man still sitting, peering at the same painting. He was, I think, even more still than before. As I neared him he stirred, stretched his arms from side to side, uncrossed his legs, and stood up. I broke the silence and said hello to this enigmatic man. He smiled a gentle smile and said hello to me. Then he sat down and patted the bench as he gestured me to join him, and we spoke for a while.

I told him that I had noticed him four hours earlier when I came into the museum and asked him if he had been sitting there all that time. He told me he had been. I asked him what he was trying to see in the painting he had been viewing for such a long time. He smiled and remained silent for a little while. Then he reached out and took my hand in his and said to me, "When you look at me, what do you see?"

I responded that I saw a very focused man. And he said that part of what he was looking for as he gazed upon the painting on the wall was the focus of the artist who had created it. And he added, "I will know the painting when I can see the soul of the artist that lives within it."

I asked him if he had seen the artist's soul and he told me he had not. He added, "But tomorrow is another day. Perhaps I will see his soul and perhaps I will not see his soul. But seeking to see his soul will perhaps show me the way to see my own." Then he released my hand, stood up, and turned to leave. He placed his hands together, bowed slightly, and spoke the last words I'm sure I will ever hear from him.

"When you stop seeking whatever it is you are seeking you are no longer alive, even if you are breathing and moving. Goodbye my friend."

And he was gone, like an apparition fading into the ether.

Out of Africa

One afternoon I came down the stairs from my office in the synagogue in Lincoln, Nebraska, and went out onto the parking lot. At the back of the parking lot, near the dumpster, was a tall Black man who had picked up an office desk we were discarding. He had it balanced on his head. I had never seen anything like that before in real life, just in some old movie, and I wondered who this out-of-place and out-of-time person could be.

I'd never seen him before. I called out to him. He paused and slowly lifted the desk from his head, turned it over, and gently lowered it to the ground. The muscles in his arms rippled as he did this. He looked apprehensive as if he thought I might not want him to take the desk, or that perhaps I would cause trouble for him. I walked over to him and extended my hand, and he reached out with both of his hands and pumped our joined hands up and down several times. When he stopped I told him that I had a friend who had a pickup truck and that I'd be glad to call him to come and help him get the desk home. But the man said it was okay, that he was used to carrying things this way.

I asked him his name and he told me it was Kwame. We stood talking for a few minutes more and I learned that he and his family were living just a few blocks away. He had come to Lincoln from Benin with help from Catholic Charities. Benin was not their home but had become their refuge when the Togolese government put a death warrant out for Kwame because of his involvement with a pro-democracy movement. He had been a member of the Togolese military, and such involvement was not acceptable for a military

Mr. Levine and Me

man. I learned that his wife's name was Akua and their children were Senan and Joel. Senan was seventeen years old and Joel was three. I asked him again if I could get him some help and he assured me that he could manage it on his own. Before he picked up the desk again I let him know that he was always welcome to come by to say hello and maybe have a cup of coffee or tea with me. He smiled an enormous, warm smile and said that he would.

Several weeks went by until I saw Kwame again. Kwame, Akua, Senan, and Joel appeared at my office to thank me for the way I had offered to help out with the moving of the desk. Akua was dressed in a colorful print garment wrapped around her like a sarong and secured with a red sash. She was an attractive person with a winning smile and perfect coffee and cream brown skin. Senan was tall and lanky and had a close resemblance to his father. Joel was small and delicate and played on the floor with a couple of toys the whole time the family was there.

They were a very likable family. They talked about some of the things they were trying to deal with as strangers in a strange land. Kwame had found a job as a machinist and had been able to do that because he was fluent in English. Senan spoke French and Evi, an Indigenous language of Togo. Akua was able to speak a little English and had an offer of employment with one of the hotels in town but was unable to accept it because of the difficulty of finding suitable childcare for Joel. While they were there I called a friend, the pastor of a nearby Presbyterian church, and asked him if the preschool at his church would take in a child from a needy family. After a little discussion, the pastor said he would make it happen. Akua was so happy that she hugged me and kissed me on the cheek. One of their problems had been solved.

A few weeks later they were reminded that they would need to find other living arrangements. The house they were living in had to be vacated because the six months of housing they had been provided had passed since they moved in, and the church that owned it wanted to ready it for another immigrant family. So Kwame and

Out of Africa

Akua, both working and earning salaries, found an apartment and let me know they would be moving in a couple of weeks. I congratulated them and told them I was happy for them.

When I returned to my home after work on the day Kwame and Akua moved to their new apartment, I was surprised to find Senan sitting on my front porch. He stood up as I approached and I noticed that he had a suitcase with him. I asked him if he was planning to travel somewhere, and he said that he wasn't. So I asked him why he was there. To my surprise he said, "I live with you now," and flashed a smile. He explained, in his broken English, that his father and mother had moved to an apartment that was not large enough for him. There was only enough room for his mother, his father, and Joel. So Senan decided that he would live with me. I had enough room in my house, so I let him move in. I mused that this must be the way it had been in Togo. If you needed a place to live you just went to someone's home and announced that you would be staying there.

A few days later I called a friend at the university and arranged for an English tutor for Senan. An education student who was fluent in French volunteered to tutor Senan and help him to better speak English. Senan was an avid student and was proficient in his new language pretty quickly. Once his English skills made it possible for him to communicate well, I called a friend who owned a wholesale food company and asked if he could take on a young man. A few days later Senan had a job working in the cut-up room, packaging fresh chicken parts for distribution to supermarkets and grocery stores around town.

Senan lived with me for several months more until he found a place of his own. Over time he rose to be foreman of the chicken cut-up room. I was very proud of him.

One evening I was at home and heard a knock at my front door. It was Akua and Kwame. Akua was holding Joel in her arms. I invited them in and began to prepare some tea. When the tea was ready we sat together in the living room and began to chat. I could sense that something was not right and I asked them to tell me what was going on.

Akua said, pointing at Kwame, "He pushed me." "Did he hurt you?" I asked. And she said he had not hurt her, but that he had pushed her. So I asked her to explain what had happened. She told me they were arguing about something and she had pushed him and he had pushed her back. I asked Kwame to explain also and he told me they had argued and she had pushed him and then he had pushed her. Kwame was a big, strapping man and Akua was a small woman. Kwame could easily hurt her. So I said to both of them that they must never do that again. Akua said she would not do that again and then added, "You tell Kwame. He will listen to you." I asked why she thought that and she said, "Because you are my father."

All of a sudden I had acquired an African daughter. I didn't know what this meant on a practical level but I spoke to Kwame and instructed him, as if I were the father of his wife, that he must not lay a hand on her again. He responded that he would not because I was her father. Kwame and Akua went on with their lives, working and becoming the Americans they wanted to be. And I still feel honored to be the "father" of Akua.

What If They're Lying?

I remember something about my grandmother's kitchen from the time when I was a little boy. She always had a collection of little metal boxes that had a coin slot on top arrayed across the shelf above the back of her stove. She called them *pushkes*. The boxes were brought by people who collected money for various local charities. They would come by once in a while to pick up their particular pushke, filled with coins, and leave an empty one in its place. This was the way it was. Every Jewish home had a few pushkes that were dropped off empty and picked up full. They were for helping various organizations that helped the poor with food, or supporting some religious activity, or raising money for the new State of Israel. All manner of charities.

The people who dropped off and picked up the pushkes were known as *schnorers*, a word that can sometimes mean something like "beggar," but which can also mean something like "charity collector." One Sunday afternoon I was at my grandparents' home when one of the schnorers arrived to pick up one of the pushkes. He took the full one for his charity and left an empty one in return. After he left, my grandfather asked my grandmother why she was always giving money to the schnorrers. "What if they're lying?" he asked.

And that brings me to another story about something that happened many years later.

I went to visit Radene, one of my synagogue members, when her father died. He had died peacefully and at the ripe old age of ninety-three. I needed to get some information that would help me as I

Mr. Levine and Me

wrote a eulogy to be presented during his funeral service that would take place the following day. Radene and I talked about her father's kindly ways, his business career, his love of his Jewish faith, his relationships with friends and family, and other aspects of his life.

Toward the end of our discussion Radene told me that she could remember only one time when her father and mother had disagreed about anything. The house her parents had lived in for all the years of their lives together was just a hundred yards or so from a railroad track, a freight line that had been turned into a bicycle path under the Rails to Trails program. In the old days, Radene told me, there were hobos who rode the freight trains and sometimes one of them would hop off the slow-moving train and panhandle along the row of houses that paralleled the railroad tracks. If one of these men came to their back door her father would invite him in, make a couple of sandwiches for him, sit with him at the kitchen table and finally send him along his way with a couple dollars.

Radene's mother was not so happy with this and she remembered one of those times that really pointed up the character of her father. She remembered her mother asking, "Why are you so nice to these hobos? You give them sandwiches any time they knock on the door." And her father answered, "They're hungry. I think it's the right thing to do." Her mother continued, "And you give them money, too." Her father responded, "They'll be hungry again." And then her mother said, "What if they're lying?" Her father paused for a few moments and finally asked, "What if they're not?"

Radene's memory of her father and my memory of my grandmother are one and the same. I remember my grandmother saying exactly the same words as Radene's father when my grandfather asked exactly the same question of his wife.

Hugs and Kisses All Around

During my second year at seminary I lived in an apartment about a twenty-minute drive from the George Washington Bridge. Every morning during the week I commuted into New York City to attend classes. Every afternoon after classes I drove about forty miles to my student congregation, where I worked as a student cantor and educator. I did this for a couple of years.

The apartment was directly across the street from the rear of a Catholic church. Down the street there was an empty old building that had once served as a convent for the nuns who were teachers at the church's school. There was just one resident in the old convent when I lived nearby, and it was not a nun. It was Father Dan Smith, who described himself as a "trouble-shooter" priest. He was a large man with a ready smile who rode a Harley Davidson motorcycle. Once I got to know him, he told me that he would only be in the neighborhood temporarily. The diocese had sent him to try and get the church across the street on track. I didn't know what the troubles with the church were, but I was glad to have met Father Dan. I once got a pretty good laugh out of him when I asked if Dan Smith was his motel name. He was a good person and we shared some nice times over coffee and conversation during the five or six months I knew him.

One day while I was at school I was asked to come to the registrar's office because I had a phone call. There were no cell phones in those days. When I picked up the phone someone from the congregation I worked with as a student cantor told me that a thirteen-year-old boy, the son of a member family, had suffered an appendicitis. The boy was brought to a hospital for what was supposed to be a routine surgery and had died on the operating table. I received that call because the Rabbi with whom I worked was on vacation in Europe and I was the nearest thing to a clergy person the congregation could call on. I wrote down the address of the family and asked the person from the congregation to let them know I'd be with them as soon as I could get there from New York. I had no idea what I was going to do once I got there. I had no experience dealing with a family's grief, let alone grief over the death of a child.

I left school and drove first to my apartment so I could change out of my jeans and sweatshirt into something more appropriate. I wondered how I was going to handle dealing with this tragedy, and then I remembered Father Dan. So I went over to the old convent. I knew he was there because his Harley was parked outside. I knocked on the door and Father Dan opened it and invited me in. I told him what had happened and that I needed some advice. He looked at me for a minute with a very serious demeanor. And then he told me that the parents of the boy who had died could not possibly be comforted so close in time to the death of their son. What they needed was to be able to express their grief, their anger, their whole range of emotions. I listened and when Father Dan stopped talking I asked him what I should do. I'll never forget the advice he gave me that day more than fifty years ago.

"When you get to their home and they let you in, give hugs and kisses all around, and then keep your stupid mouth shut."

When I arrived at the home of that very sad family I followed the advice, the instruction, of that priest who had become my friend and my mentor. I rang the bell. Somebody let me in. I hugged and kissed the grieving mother and father and then spent the next hour and a half listening as they poured their hearts out, bared their souls, opened themselves completely.

Hugs and Kisses All Around

The following day I conducted the funeral service for the family. It was the first funeral service I'd ever officiated, and I think it was the most difficult one I've ever led in my half century of communal Jewish life. The outpouring of the family the day before was the basis of the eulogy I delivered. I saw this family a few times after that day until the dean of the seminary suggested that I move on to a different student position in another part of New Jersey so that I could gain wider experience. So I moved on.

More than twenty years later I received a letter from the mother of that young boy who had died so tragically. She had somehow tracked me down and gotten the address of the synagogue I was serving. Her letter brought back memories of my first funeral service, of my early experience with such an extreme level of grief. When I read how grateful that mother was for the kind words of comfort and care I had provided at a most terrible time for her family, I was also reminded of Father Dan Smith who had advised me, "hugs and kisses all around, and keep your stupid mouth shut." I had followed that advice and hadn't said much of anything when I visited with that family. Somehow the mother remembered her own outpouring of grief and sadness as words I had spoken on that terrible day. It was her own thoughts, her own words, that ultimately had comforted her.

Thinking about it now, I guess Dan Smith, Catholic priest, was one of my best rabbis.

From the Children of America to the Children of India

When I was about ten or eleven years old I met Miss Maskel, the best teacher I ever knew. Miss Maskel was a short but stately woman with dark hair and a ruddy complexion. She often wore a colorful sari with a sash around her waist. One of the features I remember was the little red dot in the middle of her forehead. I thought she was a Hindu for a long time but at some point learned that she was Jewish and had assumed an Indian look to better teach her class about India.

Miss Maskel (her name was Anna but I would never have called her by her first name) was part of a special program in which fifth- and sixth-grade students were to stay with the same teacher for both of those school years (I think Yale University had something to do with that program). She was also, I realized much later, a very courageous person. In those days it was mandated that each school day had to begin with the recitation of the Pledge of Allegiance, followed by the Lord's Prayer. Miss Maskel began class by asking us to stand. Then she said, each and every day, "I've been instructed by the Board of Education to lead the class in the Pledge of Allegiance and the Lord's Prayer. Those who choose to not recite one or both of these may remain silent."

From the Children of America to the Children of India

I didn't know how important that was at the time. Miss Maskel risked losing her job every day by saying those few words. In later years I knew that she didn't think it was proper to ask children who might not be Christian to recite a specifically Christian prayer. It was a quiet lesson in speaking truth to power and acceptance of differences.

In the beginning of my fifth-grade year Miss Maskel announced that we were going to have a unit on India. One part of that unit would include the writing of a radio play about the life of children in America for the children of India. Part of our preparation for that project included learning about the different cultures that were all around us all the time. African American, Italian American, Chinese American, Polish American, Jewish American, Ukrainian American and more. From time to time we were asked to bring something to school from our homes that reflected whichever culture our families sprang from. Sometimes it was objects and other times special foods. I remember bringing a roasting pan filled with holubtsi, or stuffed cabbage rolls, on one of those occasions. Once in a while parents or grandparents would visit and tell stories about "the old country." None of us fifth graders knew that Miss Maskel was teaching us the art of tolerance. She knew, and quietly imparted her knowledge, that it's difficult to hate, or even dislike, those who are different if you get to know them. It was a good lesson.

All during the fifth-grade year, as we learned about cultures different than our own, we every so often would write brief stories about things in our lives that would later be included in our radio play.

Toward the end of the school year we arrived at our classroom and were greeted by the AV cart. There were microphones with little screens to block the sound of breathing. And there was a very large reel-to-reel tape recorder, something kids today may have never seen. Miss Maskel had rounded up someone who was going to serve as sound engineer. The stories we'd written had been organized, edited, and typewritten so that we would be able to read them easily.

Then we made the recording. It was about an hour in length and we were all very proud and excited about what we had done.

The very last week of school that year, Miss Maskel asked us to dress in our best clothes the following day because we were going to have some important guests. She didn't tell us who the guests were, but all of us were excited about it.

The next day when we arrived at Miss Maskel's classroom we went through our usual opening rituals, reciting or not reciting the Pledge of Allegiance and the Lord's Prayer. On each of our desks was a sheet of ruled notebook paper. Miss Maskel told us that our guests would be arriving soon and she wanted us to write welcoming notes. She said our guests were coming down from New York and that they were representatives of the Indian Government who were part of India's United Nations delegation. None of the kids thought to ask how Miss Maskel had managed to make that happen. We all got busy writing our notes and when we were finished we passed them to the front. Miss Maskel read each of them aloud and thanked us for having done such a good job.

Finally our guests arrived. There were three men and two women. The men were dressed in business suits and the women in colorful saris. To all of us children they seemed very exotic and yet, because of the studies we had done that year, somehow also familiar. One of the women, who seemed to be the leader of the group, spoke to us and thanked us for our efforts in learning about India and for having created the radio play. Then we all listened to the radio play, which began with Miss Maskel saying, "From the Children of America to the Children of India," followed by our own voices speaking in turn about what it was like to be a child living in America.

When the recording came to its end the room fell silent. After a few seconds one of the Indian men stood and said something like, "Thank you, children. We will be delighted to share what you have done with the children of India." Then our guests put their hands together, bowed slightly, and said in unison, "Namaste."

That was almost the end of this story, but not quite.

From the Children of America to the Children of India

We returned to school to begin the sixth-grade school year in the same classroom with the same teacher, Miss Maskel. We began that first day of school in the same way we had begun each school day the previous year, but then Miss Maskel held up a letter and said she would like to read it to us. It was from one of the people from the Indian delegation to the United Nations who had visited with us at the end of the previous school year. The letter once again thanked us and added that our radio play had been translated into many of India's languages. It would be played in schools all across that country.

I think that each of us had made a multitude of friends we would never get to meet.

There's yet another piece to this story about Miss Maskel.

When I finished the sixth grade I moved on with life. I went to junior high school and high school and then enlisted in the Army. I never saw Miss Maskel during those years. After I was discharged from the Army I was home for a visit and was walking down a street where I'd spent a good part of my childhood. I heard a voice calling out, "Michael Weisser!" I turned and there was Miss Maskel. She looked the same except for her hair, which had gone from black to gray, and the little red dot on her forehead was gone. She was not wearing a sari but rather a tailored dress and jacket.

As I approached she opened her arms and greeted me happily with a hug. We went into a luncheonette and sat there for an hour or so talking and drinking coffee. It was a beautiful time as we recalled our fifth- and sixth-grade experience together almost a decade earlier. Miss Maskel had retired from teaching and was now spending her time writing and being involved in civil rights activities. When it came time for us to go on our ways, Miss Maskel gave me her card and said she hoped we would stay in touch.

When I got settled after the next phase of my life, five or six years later, I came across her card and sent her a letter. A few weeks later I received her response. We continued this correspondence two or three times a year for the next thirty years. In 2002, I wrote to Miss

Maskel from New Zealand to tell her that I would be working there for the next three years. I remember writing that I thought I would retire afterwards and that I felt blessed to be able to wind down my career in such a beautiful place. I never received an answer.

About a year after I wrote that letter I received a phone call from the United States. The woman who called explained to me that she had been a volunteer secretary and assistant to Miss Maskel for several years and that when Miss Maskel died peacefully, the task of sorting through her things had fallen to her. While doing that task she came across the last letter I had written and told me it had arrived in the last days of Miss Maskel's life. She also told me she had found a book of Miss Maskel's poetry that had been signed and inscribed to me. The young woman told me she would mail it to me. It arrived a couple of weeks later.

I cried when I read the inscription from Miss Maskel. It read: "I always knew you'd make it!"

He'd Want to Be Buried in His Uniform

Mr. Michael was a true son of Tennessee. He was a burly man with a winning personality. His speech was filled with southernisms. Expressions like, "I'll tell you what . . ." and "I'm gonna show you the way the cow ate the cabbage . . ." and "There's gonna be trouble in the camp . . ." rolled off his tongue like water in a stream flowing over the rocks. Everyone who knew him liked him, and I think he liked everyone he knew. He owned a full-service gas station when I knew him, and for him his customers were always the boss. He catered to them and took good care of their cars. Because of who he was, his auto repair business was always busy.

I remember the first time I stopped at Mr. Michael's Esso station (that was in the days before the name change to Exxon). His driveway man, a slight black fellow who carried himself with authority, was wearing his blue trousers and shirt with the Esso logo above one pocket and his name, Pete, above the other. Pete pumped my gas, squeegeed the windshield, checked the oil, and accepted payment for my gasoline. He said goodbye and wished me a good day. I saw Pete many times after that because Mr. Michael's gas station became my first choice for gasoline and service. After a while Pete began to feel like an old friend to me. I could tell he was an old friend of Mr. Michael's, too. Whenever they were in the same place there was always some friendly banter going on. It was not like employee/employer talk, but something more personal, more real.

Mr. Levine and Me

I remember Mr. Michael telling me that Pete had worked for him for many years. He described Pete in terms that could have applied to a brother. Pete, he told me, was usually very reliable, but every now and then he would start hitting the bottle and get drunk enough to get himself in trouble. Mr. Michael told me he had bailed Pete out of jail numerous times. He smiled when he told me that he always warned Pete that it was the last time he would do that. "I'll tell you what," he'd tell Pete at such times, "next time I'm gonna let you rot in that jail." But when the next time came Mr. Michael again came to the rescue any time of night or day. He told me that he and his wife sometimes had Pete and his wife over for a holiday dinner. Even though I was a newcomer to Memphis, I already knew that having your Black driveway man and his wife over for a holiday dinner was not something many people would ever do. As I said, the relationship between these two men was like the relationship between brothers who may have taken different paths of life.

About a year after my first encounter with Pete, I stopped into the gas station and there was a different driveway man. He did the same job Pete had always done, pumping gas, checking the oil, and cleaning the windshield. I asked this newcomer where Pete was, and he told me that Pete had died a couple weeks before. I felt a wave of sadness when I heard this. I had really come to like Pete and I think he had come to like me as well. I always called him by his name and he always called me by my name. We had grown, over time, in the depth of our momentary meetings. Pete was a real person to me and I to him, I believe.

Because of the feelings I had for Pete I wanted to learn what had happened to him, and so I went into the garage looking for Mr. Michael. I found him in his office and asked if he had a minute. He gestured to a chair and offered me a cup of coffee, which I accepted. After we had exchanged a few words, I told him I was sad to hear Pete had died and I asked him what had happened. Mr. Michael told me that Pete had gotten pancreatic cancer and had only lived a few weeks after it was diagnosed. I sensed a very heavy sadness in Mr.

He'd Want to Be Buried in His Uniform

Michael as he related how difficult it had been to spend time with his old friend Pete as he lay dying. When Pete finally breathed his last, Mr. Michael assured Pete's wife that he would take care of any funeral expenses. And at that point in the conversation Mr. Michael told me something that caused both of us to laugh out loud.

"When I was discussing the funeral arrangements with Pete's wife, she told me, 'He'd want to be buried in his uniform,'" he said. "And I told her I didn't know Pete had served in the military." 'Oh no, Julian,' she said. 'Pete was never in the Army. I'm talking about his Esso uniform. He was so proud to wear it every day for all those years, and so proud that you were his friend, no matter what.'"

Look up: What Do You See?

One day I got a call from the wife of an old friend. My old friend had succumbed to cancer and his funeral, in accordance with traditional Jewish custom, would take place the next afternoon. She understood that I might not be able to make it to New York in time, but she hoped it would somehow be possible. I took down the details and told her I would try to be there. I was living in Lincoln, Nebraska, at the time and the next flight to New York would not be until early the next morning. I booked a flight with a stop and a plane change in Chicago and thought I'd probably be able to make it on time. Of course there was a bit of a delay in Chicago. What else is new?

When I arrived at LaGuardia I got a car service and told the driver to get me to the funeral home as soon as possible. The service was set to begin in a little over half an hour. The driver did his best but by the time we arrived outside Riverside Chapel in Manhattan it was already well past the time at which the funeral service for my friend had been scheduled. I got out of the car and asked the driver to wait. When I went inside I spoke with one of the funeral directors and he told me the service had ended a few minutes earlier and that the family and the hearse had left for the cemetery that was located about thirty miles out on Long Island. The man I had spoken to was kind enough to come outside and give the car service driver the information he needed to get me to the cemetery. And off we went.

Look up: What Do You See?

Once we got to the cemetery I ran into the office near the entrance to find out where in the cemetery my friend's burial would take place. The driver brought me there and I got out of the car and walked to where there was a group of men dressed in the Hasidic manner, black suits and felt hats. My friend's wife and several other people were also there standing beside the open grave. As I approached it was clear to me which of the Hasidic men would be leading the ritual, and I told him I was sorry to be late. I also told him I did not have a kippah, the head covering that many Jews wear during religious ritual and that some wear all the time out of, as they believe, respect for God. The rabbi (I never learned his name) looked at me and said, "Are you Jewish?" I answered "Yes." And he went on, "You don't have a yarmulke?" I said no, and that I hoped no one would be offended.

He looked at me for a moment. He was smiling. Then he said, "Look up. What do you see?" I looked up and there was nothing to see. So I said, "I see the sky." The rabbi, orthodox to his core, one who would never be without a head covering, smiled and said, "You see the most beautiful kippah there can be, given to you as a gift from God." He put his arm around my shoulders and walked with me to the graveside, then began the burial service, he in his black hat and me with the sky for a yarmulke.

In the quiet of my mind I uttered the sweetest "Amen" I could muster.

Roses Are Red...

One Friday evening as I was leading a Sabbath service, a stranger entered the sanctuary. He was tall and gaunt. He looked to be thirty-five or forty years old. His face was like a sculpture of sharp angles. He had a ruddy complexion and a shock of reddish-brown hair. He took a seat near the front of the sanctuary and seemed to be lost in thought as he sat there. He stood up when the others around him did so and sat back down when they did until near the end of the service, when the Kaddish, the memorial prayer, is recited in memory of those who have died. After those words he remained standing, a smile on his face, and he remained standing until one of the members of the synagogue went over to him and told him he could be seated. He looked a little perplexed, but he sat down and gazed toward the front in silence.

Each Friday evening that followed for about the next month this enigmatic man returned, took his place in the same seat, and listened to the words and music of the service. He always left when the service concluded and did not join with the assembled people when they went to the social hall for refreshments and socializing.

The woman, Marcia, who had let him know he could be seated on his first visit, began to sit beside him each week. She was a long-time member of the synagogue who served on the Board of Trustees and headed a couple of the committees that helped to run the affairs of the congregation. She was also a clinical social worker and recognized something in this man who had appeared in our midst. On one occasion the man, who we now knew was called Royce, stood up during the service and began to recite the words of Hail Mary from the Catholic tradition. I was thankful that no one interrupted him, as it was pretty clear that he probably didn't know he was in a synagogue rather than in a church. When he was finished he remained standing, and as I began to continue with the liturgy of that evening, Marcia approached and whispered something to him. Then the two of them left through the nearest exit.

I later learned that Marcia had asked him if he would like to go and get some ice cream. And that's what they had done. They took a walk down the street to a nearby market and Marcia bought each of them a pint of ice cream. When Marcia returned, Royce was not with her, and she told me he had decided to go home. She also told me that it was clear from her conversation with him that he suffered with some kind of mental illness. She said he had told her that he visited with a psychiatrist regularly and was taking medication that helped him to live a normal life. Marcia had told Royce he was always welcome to return and tried to gently explain that synagogues were different than churches.

Royce returned the following week and continued attending on Friday evenings. Over time he began to have conversations with some of the members and with me. These conversations were more likely to happen when Marcia was around, but sometimes Royce would talk with people even when she was not present. After a couple months, Royce began to come to the social time that followed each service. He seemed to enjoy being with the people in an informal setting and little by little he became relaxed in the company of his new friends.

During one of those gatherings in the social hall, Royce approached me and said that he had heard the announcement about the service and study session that took place on Saturday mornings. He asked if it would be all right if he came. I told him it would be okay, and he smiled. The following morning Royce was there for Torah study. The session began with an informal service, with everyone seated around tables that had been pushed together to form a big rectangle. About thirty or so people regularly attended. Royce

Mr. Levine and Me

took a seat next to Marcia and followed along without ever saying anything. He continued attending for a long time.

About two or three weeks after Royce began coming to the Saturday morning services and study sessions I got a call from his father. His father told me that Royce had let him know that he was attending services and he wanted to be sure that it was all right with the folks at the synagogue that a Catholic, a man who had certain issues, was coming regularly. I told him it was not a problem, and he explained to me that Royce sometimes acted out and made people uncomfortable. I assured him that it was not a problem. His father thanked me again and told me that if any problems arose I should give him a call. I told him I would do that and again mentioned that it was no problem for Royce to be there.

Royce kept attending on Saturdays and over time even participated a little. One Saturday as we were going over some text, one of the people at the table said she had brought a poem that she thought was relevant to the bit of Torah we were studying that week. She asked me if it would be okay for her to recite it, and I of course said yes. She stood up and read a lovely poem that was indeed relevant, and when she finished everyone around the table gave her a round of applause.

At that point Royce raised his hand and said, "I have a poem, too. May I recite it?" I told him that of course he could recite his poem. So Royce stood up and said:

Roses are red,
Violets are blue,
I'm schizophrenic.
And so am I.

There was a palpable silence in the room until finally someone laughed, and the laughter grew to a happy crescendo. Everyone was laughing and applauding. I looked at Royce and never have I seen such a magnificent smile on anyone before. In that moment I knew that Royce was completely accepted by the group of people at the synagogue, but more importantly, I knew that Royce knew he was completely accepted by them.

I looked at Marcia, and she was beaming!

Rosetta Stone

I was working in Sacramento, serving a congregation there as Cantor and Educator. It was a pleasant place to work. The community was small enough for me to know most of the people and large enough to keep things interesting. When I first arrived there I needed to hire a secretary because the previous secretary had moved on before my arrival. I placed ads in the local media and soon I had a pile of résumés on my desk. I sorted through them and took a pass on most for one reason or another until finally I had three that seemed to be from qualified people. Then I began the process of interviewing these people, the final three.

Two of them were women and one was a man. Each of them was a competent person. Each had a good work history and positive references. I wished I could have hired all of them. I was faced with a real dilemma. As I began arranging for interviews I felt a sense of relief when one of the applicants, the man, let me know that he had accepted another position. So I was down to two equally qualified people.

During the interview one of the things I asked each of the remaining two persons was why they had left their previous jobs. The first explained that there was no room for growth in her job and that she wanted to work in a situation with more responsibility. That seemed reasonable to me.

When it came time to interview the second person, Rosetta, her answer to that question was that she had loved her job. She had been working in Denver as executive assistant to the president of a local bank. It was a good job, she said, but she had to leave it for personal

Rosetta Stone

reasons. When I asked if she would be comfortable telling me more about that, she told me that she needed to be in Sacramento because her mother had fallen ill and she needed to be with her, needed to take care of her. I was so impressed with her spirit of kindness and love toward her mother. These were some of the qualities that would be a perfect fit for a person working at a synagogue. Whoever worked as the secretary there would be the first person any member or visitor would encounter when they came to the synagogue.

And then I asked her why her mother had chosen the name Rosetta for her. Rosetta told me that her mother had once, before she was born, taken a trip to Egypt, seen the pyramids and did all the tourist things that people do when they visit Egypt. When she got home from that trip she began reading everything she could get her hands on about Egypt. When she came across the story of the Rosetta Stone and learned how it had enabled researchers to decipher ancient Egyptian hieroglyphics, she named her daughter after it. As Rosetta grew up, her mother told her that, like the Rosetta Stone, she would someday be the key to opening up that which was hidden, and that would allow her to learn the secrets that would help her to live a good life. She told me that whenever she came up against something that seemed incapable of solution, she remembered her mother's words and persevered until she solved whatever mystery or problem was before her.

I hired Rosetta that day, and although I moved on after several years, Rosetta remained for a long time as the first one anyone encountered when they visited that community.

Joe from Petaluma and Grandpa the Goat Farmer

I was in my office at the Sacramento synagogue when Rosetta brought in a person who wanted to speak with me. His name was Joe and he told me that he and his family, who would be moving to Sacramento soon, were looking for a synagogue with which they could affiliate. I walked with him around the building, pointing out the sanctuary, chapel, classrooms, and community garden. We returned to my office, sat and chatted for a while, and I told Joe that I hoped he and his family would soon become a part of our community. He said they probably would do so and stood up to leave. I walked with him to the exit and, almost as an afterthought, I asked him where he was moving from. He answered, "Petaluma."

A bell went off in my head. My grandfather Frank, with whom the family had lost touch many years before, was last known to be in Petaluma, where he was living on a goat farm. I asked Joe if he had always lived in Petaluma, and he said he was born and raised there. I went on and asked if he had ever known an old guy named Frank Weisser, my long-lost grandfather, and he told me that he didn't remember anyone by that name. But he also told me that there was a store there where lots of old guys hung out. The place had a back room with a couple of card tables and a coffee pot and there were always some old guys hanging out. Maybe one of them might remember him. He gave me the name of the street it was on and then he left.

Joe from Petaluma and Grandpa the Goat Farmer

After Joe left I was filled with a swirl of memories from long ago, from a time when I was maybe nine or ten years old. I remembered Grandpa Frank and Grandma Pearl. Grandma Pearl was a typical yiddishe mama, short and stout with permed graying hair and an overabundance of makeup and bright-red lipstick that she reveled in smearing on the cheeks of anyone who came into range. She always had piles of cookies and other sweets around, and her home was a very welcoming place. Grandpa Frank was a quiet man who was very proud of his heritage as a German Jew. His family had come to America in the 1800s long before the tragedy that befell Germany and the world in the twentieth century. He always insisted that the children in the family pronounce his name with a German accent. "My name is not *Frank*, it's *Franc*!" he would say, and add that our family name was not pronounced *Weisser* but rather *Veisser*.

He owned a commercial laundry business and he and Grandma Pearl lived a comfortable life as a result. They had two sons, my father Louis and my uncle Julius. My father never went to college and he worked as a bus driver for the Connecticut Company. Julius had graduated from Yale and worked for the State Department in Washington.

One day, after many years of marriage, Grandpa Frank announced to Grandma Pearl that he was going to leave her. He had sold the laundry company and turned most of the proceeds of that sale over to Grandma Pearl. And he had gotten a pickup truck on which he built a little peaked-roof house, complete with a wood-burning stove. Maybe it was the first RV. At any rate, my grandparents were divorced, and Grandpa drove away in his homemade camper.

Nobody heard from Grandpa Frank for the next few years until my sister was about to be married. Apparently he had been in touch with someone in the family, because he contacted my sister and asked if he could attend her wedding. She of course agreed, and from out of nowhere Grandpa Frank appeared on the day of the wedding, which was held in the ballroom of a hotel in downtown New Haven. I remember people commenting on how strange it

Mr. Levine and Me

was that he sat with Grandma Pearl during the wedding. He stayed around for a few days and then was gone again. He never returned, but during his visit he told people that he was happy living near Petaluma, California, where he had bought a goat farm.

Two or three years later Grandma Pearl moved away, too, I think to Washington, D.C. to be with her son, my uncle Julius. As a result I never got to know her well or to have a real relationship with her.

I mulled all this over for a couple of weeks and then decided I would go to Petaluma and see if there were any traces of my grandfather to be found. It was less than a two-hour drive from Sacramento to Petaluma. When I got there I found the store Joe had mentioned, and sure enough there were a few old guys hanging out in the back room drinking coffee, smoking cigarettes, and playing cards. One of the men asked me if I needed something, and I asked the group if anyone had known an old guy named Frank Weisser who had lived around there since sometime in the early fifties. After a few minutes someone remembered my grandfather and said, "I remember him. That was that Jewish guy who used to sell goat cheese to the I-talians." Some of the other men said they remembered him too. I asked if anyone knew what had become of him and someone said they thought he had died maybe fifteen or so years ago. And then, amazingly to me, one of the men said that he knew where he was buried and asked me if I would like to see his grave. I told him I would and I asked for directions, but the man said he'd be glad to take me there. I thought that was a great kindness.

We drove in my new friend's car for about half an hour and came to a road that ran behind some rural properties. There was a small burial plot near the road, well away from the buildings on the other side of the property. I thought it must have been an old family burial place like the ones I'd seen in other places.

We got out of the car and walked to where the mini-cemetery was. And there, to my amazement and somehow a feeling of joy, was a headstone with the name Franc Weisser and the date November 8, 1966, engraved in the stone. Someone knew his preference about his name. I didn't recognize any of the names on the other headstones and I had no idea who might have erected this memorial to the grandfather I didn't really know. I felt happy that someone had done so. I will always be grateful for my chance meeting with Joe and his mention of Petaluma that brought me to this place.

The Whole World Would Be Pretty

When I first came to Memphis I was always confused getting around. It was a big, bustling city with heavy traffic everywhere and, to me at least, a confusing interstate loop around the city. Sometimes I-240 is north and sometimes east, west, or south. It took me quite a while to figure it out.

I remember once when I was out looking for Getwell Road, a north/south street, and I found myself on I-240 West on the north side of town. I passed exit after exit but there was no Getwell Road where I thought it should be. Finally I decided to get off of I-240 and find someone who could give me directions.

As I came off the exit ramp I found myself in a pretty run-down neighborhood. There was trash in some of the front yards and many of the houses were obviously in a state of disrepair. I had been on Getwell Road before, and it hadn't been like this. So I decided to get back on the interstate and keep looking for Getwell Road. I soon discovered that the ramp that should have gotten me back on the interstate was closed. So I started zigzagging on the neighborhood streets trying to keep the interstate in view. The neighborhood kept getting more and more run down, and here and there were small groups of mostly young men, tough looking young men, on some of the street corners. They didn't look like people I wanted to ask for directions, so I kept on zigzagging my way through the neighborhood.

The Whole World Would Be Pretty

After a few minutes I turned a corner, and there in the midst of this run-down neighborhood was a nice house. It looked freshly painted. There were flower beds against the front of the house, and the lawn was green and trimmed. There was an elderly Black man sitting on the porch and I thought this was a person who would help me to find my way. I pulled up to the curb and started to walk over to speak with this man. He stood up as I approached. He was about my size, probably twice my age, but he looked to be in better shape. I remember he was wearing a pair of bib overalls over a plaid shirt.

As I neared he said, "You looking for the on ramp?" I answered that I was and asked him how he knew. He told me lots of people continued to come through since they closed the old on ramp. He told me I'd be okay, that I should just go straight two blocks, take a right, and the ramp would be right there. I asked him where Getwell Road was. He smiled and told me I was on the wrong side of town. He told me to just follow the loop around and it would go south and then east and pretty soon I'd see an exit for Getwell Road.

I thanked that nice man a couple of times until he waved me off and said it was no problem. I started to walk back to my car, but then I turned back and spoke again to the man in the bib overalls.

"Is this your house?" I asked, and he replied, "Yes it is." I said, "It sure is pretty." He said thanks and then walked over to me, put his arm around my shoulders, and said, "You know, son, if everybody took care of their own little place, the whole world would be pretty."

I've thought about that many times over the years. Every time I plant flowers around my house I remember his words and take them to heart: "If everybody took care of their own little place, the whole world would be pretty."

Now That's Gifted

Remember when school boards instituted what they called "gifted programs?" It was always a bad idea in my opinion.

Its main result was to create a kind of caste system in our schools. Parents pushed for their children to be selected for these programs. Kids were urged to study day and night in order to get their grades up to a point where they would be eligible to be selected for these gifted programs. Those who were selected were segregated into classes with so-called advanced curricula. Overnight they became darlings of the school systems and in many cases targets aimed at by other students who had not made the cut. Parents began to live vicariously through their children, the way that soccer moms and Little League or Pop Warner League dads did when their children were on the athletic fields. It always struck me as a little strange.

Some kids who were not really interested in being involved in various sports were coaxed and cajoled by eager parents to take part and then were pressured to be the best kid on the field. Moms and dads who were usually just regular parents would sometimes get into fights with other moms and dads over the call of a referee or an umpire. Their children were being pushed into becoming little professional players, but it was the parents who took on the glory of a child's base hit or of a goal they scored. It seemed to me that oftentimes the children were simply proxies for the egos of their parents. And that's the way things evolved as the schools' gifted programs stumbled along.

There were many such parents in my community, and I understood, somewhat, the depth of their feelings as they touted their

Now That's Gifted

children's accomplishments. There was one mom in particular who constantly reminded everyone she spoke with that her son was in the gifted program. She'd put her hand on his shoulder and say, "He's in the gifted program." Her son always looked uncomfortable at such times. I held my tongue for quite a while until I couldn't stand it anymore.

One day, as her son and I were being subjected to the vicarious pride being displayed by this mom, I interrupted her with a question. "Have you ever heard of Mozart?" I asked. And she responded curtly that of course she had heard of Mozart. I went on. "Did you know that Mozart was performing on keyboard instruments and violins when he was five years old and had played before European royalty at that tender age?" She said she didn't know about that, and I went on. "Did you know that Mozart composed a fully orchestrated symphony when he was just eight years old in 1761?" I knew these things because some of my studies had to do with music and music history.

The mom fell silent and just looked at me quizzically. Finally I said, "Now that's gifted. Your son is a wonderful child. He's a good reader, he's very intelligent, but he's not Mozart. You're doing him a disservice by what you are doing. Let him be a child. He only gets to be a child once." She frowned and walked away, her son's hand in hers.

A couple weeks later she made an appointment to come and speak with me. I thought she was probably angry with me and wanted to express that anger. I waited in my office for her to arrive. I must admit I felt a little trepidation. When she arrived she sat across my desk from me and with a slight smile on her face thanked me for what I had done.

"You made me think about what I was doing. I know now that I was taking pride away from my son. If there was any pride it belonged to him, not to me. I won't do that again. I just want him to be my little boy. Thank you."

Mr. Levine and Me

After she had gone I thought about her visit. It must have taken a good measure of courage for her to come in and say what she had said to me. The words I had spoken to her about her son came into my mind about her as I thought, "Now that's gifted."

God Has Left the Room

Every Saturday morning thirty or forty of my congregants joined me sitting around tables that had been pushed together in a big rectangle. They were there for an abbreviated Shabbat service that was followed by an hour or so of Torah study. It was a good time for all. Each week I would bake challah and maybe strudel, and I sometimes thought that folks turned up more for the baked goods than for the service or study session.

    The service portion of the morning was conducted by everyone because after a while everyone knew the liturgy almost by heart. It began at ten o'clock and usually lasted for about thirty or forty minutes. Following the service we'd take a break for coffee, challah, and something sweet like my strudel or perhaps some cookies or pastries that other folks had brought along. Once everyone had their fill of coffee and sweets we would all return to our seats around the table and talk about some part of the Torah until noon. I found it interesting that people almost always sat in the same place around the table each week. After we finished up, we'd say, "so long" and Shabbat Shalom and leave, knowing we'd be meeting again the following Saturday. After a while, the people who attended became Saturday-morning friends. Very few of them saw one another during the week, and Saturday mornings became, in addition to worship and study, a time to reconnect with people who had become important to each other, at least on a once-a-week basis. I loved that time together each week. It was really very special to me.

    There was one person who was a regular attendee. She came to be with the group every Saturday morning but always arrived late, just in time for coffee and refreshments. She was one of those people to whom it was difficult to assign an age. She could have been thirty-five or so, or maybe forty, or perhaps forty-five. She was short and plain looking and she had a large-toothed smile almost perpetually on her face. She brightened up whatever room she entered. Her name was Lisa and she usually sat next to a woman named Wendy, a small, slight person who was always involved in one social action project or another. Oftentimes, once the study session ended, Lisa and Wendy would leave together and go to their favorite vegetarian restaurant for lunch. I went with them a few times, as did a few others from the Saturday morning group.

As I got to know Lisa I learned that she was Jewish. You wouldn't think I'd need to learn that since the service and study session took place at my synagogue, but we were always open to all comers, and there was usually a mixture of people sitting around the table: Jewish, Christian, White, Black, Latino, Gay and Straight. Although Lisa was Jewish, she was not a synagogue-goer. She attended a Unitarian/Universalist church on a regular basis, and she once told me she did so because she was not comfortable with "the god stuff." That was okay with me, and really understandable too. After all I was a rabbi, and I was sometimes uncomfortable with the god stuff, too.

I once told Lisa that she didn't have to come late. She could come during the service segment of our Saturday-morning gathering and just enjoy the chanting and poetry of the service without having to worry about the god stuff. But she declined. It was several months before I realized that Lisa, if she thought the service was still going on when she arrived, would sit out on the stoop until she was sure that it was time to move on to the study part of the morning. I never said anything to her about this, but I did think I'd like to get her to change her mind and be fully a part of the group that met every Saturday morning.

One Saturday morning we concluded the service around those tables a little early. Everyone was up getting their coffee and cake or challah when I went outside for a breath of fresh air, and there was Lisa, sitting there on the stoop. I sat down beside her and she asked me why I was outside so early. The service, she knew, should have been going for at least another ten or fifteen minutes. I stood up and told her we had finished early that day, and then I added, "It's okay to come in now. God has left the room." The smile on her face grew to enormous proportions and she laughed out loud. So did I.

 Lisa remained uncomfortable with the god stuff, but every once in a while she'd come in before the service ended and take her regular seat. We never spoke of it again and I never learned just why Lisa was uncomfortable with the god stuff. She was a good person, and that was good enough for me.

Preach It Brother

Just about every year on Martin Luther King Day it was my practice to observe the importance of the man and his message with a special gathering at whichever synagogue I was serving. Over time the program for that special occasion evolved into a series of talks by community leaders of various traditions, interspersed with pieces of music. I always delivered a message of peace and harmony, along with some of the teachings of Dr. King, during these events. We always concluded these programs, from the earliest to the latest, with the singing of "Lift Every Voice and Sing," which some folks think of as the Black National Anthem, and "We Shall Overcome," which we sang with everyone's arms crossed in front of them and hands held by those next to them in a long human chain that circled around the sanctuary and up and down the center aisle. It was always a wonderful conclusion to the event.

MLK Day always takes place on the Monday closest to his birthday, which is January 15th. Because most churches, especially African American churches, observed it on that Monday, I opted early on for my synagogue's observance to be the day before, on Sunday afternoon, so that I wouldn't compete with other celebrations that might be happening. As a result I was available to participate in the churches as well as in the synagogue.

I came out of retirement in 2008 to work with a Flushing, New York synagogue, and a couple years later I met the new pastor of the Macedonian African Methodist Episcopal Church, a historic congregation that had been founded in 1811 by freed slaves. Rev. Richard McEachern and I talked a few times and it was in 2014 that he asked me to give a sermon at his church on MLK Day. Of course I agreed to do it. There were only a few days between the time he asked me to participate and MLK Day itself, so I got busy and put together a sermon for the occasion.

There was a fly in the ointment, though. On the Thursday prior to the MLK Day weekend, during which I had a major program planned for my synagogue and was scheduled to speak at Macedonian A.M.E. Church, I began to have some troubling symptoms. I was having a hard time walking up even a few stairs. My breathing was sometimes very labored, I had a tightness in my chest, and I was feeling very weak. Everything seemed difficult to do. I was in overall good health, I thought, but I had a pacemaker that was first implanted in 1990 to take care of what the doctors told me was a "right bundle branch block." I thought the symptoms I was experiencing had to be somehow related to that. So I went, without an appointment, to the arrhythmia clinic that was taking care of monitoring my pacemaker and asked them to check it out for me. They did, and determined there was nothing wrong with the pacemaker. I remembered while I was there that I had on a couple of occasions in the past experienced unexplained bouts of anemia and so I asked if blood work could be done. Fortunately, there was a lab in the building and my electrophysiologist ordered the appropriate tests. I went home not feeling any better and wondered what was going on.

About ten o'clock that evening I got a call from the doctor, who told me that I was severely anemic. He told me he had made an appointment with a hematologist for eight o'clock the following morning and that it was imperative that I keep that appointment. In the morning I made my way to the hematologist's office and got nervous when I saw the sign on the building: "Hematology - Oncology."

Anyway, I went into the office and was seen right away. The doctor (a no-nonsense Korean woman), once she'd done a preliminary test or two, said that I was in a dangerous place and should go to the hospital to be treated. I explained that I had a major event at my synagogue on Sunday and had to be there, and the next day another major event at the church, which coincidentally was just a half block away from this doctor's office. I asked if there was any way she could keep me safe over the weekend. She thought about it for a couple minutes and finally said she thought she could.

I was ushered into a room filled with recliner chairs, many of which were filled with people receiving chemotherapy, and I began to get liquid iron pumped into my veins. It took an hour or two to complete the process and when it was finished the Doctor said, "I think you will be okay for the weekend, but if you have any symptoms you must go to the hospital." She asked me what time I would be finished at the church on Monday, and I told her it would probably be around noon. She told me that the minute I was finished there I should come back to her office, and I said that I would. She reminded me again to scrap everything if I had any symptoms and also that if my red cell count was very low on Monday, I'd have to be hospitalized to get things under control.

On Sunday, the program at the synagogue went off well. All the people I'd invited to participate, representatives from the African American, Muslim, Jewish, and Sikh communities, along with a politician or two, showed up and did their part with readings, music, and brief talks. I delivered a message to the group and we concluded with "We Shall Overcome," as I'd done for many years. I felt weak and tired but not as much as before I'd had the iron infusion.

And then it was Monday. I arrived at the church at a quarter to nine, went in, and found Rev. McEachern. We chatted for a few minutes and I let him know what was going on with me. He said it would be all right if I bowed out, and he'd explain to the congregation if I did. I told him I thought I was okay and that I'd be going to the doctor's office right after the service.

At nine the service began. The band started playing, the organist cranked up his instrument, and the gospel choir came in singing, everyone clapping their hands above their heads, weaving their way down the aisles, and making a very joyful noise! Rev. McEachern led the community and acted as a sort of emcee moving things along. One of the elders of the church spoke for a few minutes.

God Has Left the Room

Somebody asked prayers for healing. The choir sang a few times and a couple of civic leaders had things to say. A group of young people from what the church called its dance ministry performed a beautiful dance specially choreographed for the occasion.

Then Rev. McEachern introduced me and concluded by saying, "Everybody, get on your feet and show Rabbi Michael a great A.M.E. welcome." There was a long period of applause as I rose from my seat. There I was, my head covered by a colorful Russian kippah, wearing a tallit, or prayer shawl, with its fringes draped over my shoulders, standing before a most wonderful congregation of people. I'd never experienced such a welcome before, and I must say it felt good.

I began my remarks slowly and deliberately. Every time I said something about Dr. King and his message the room filled with the sounds of Amen and Hallelujah and ripples of applause. Every now and then the organist played a few random chords to punctuate whatever it was I had said. As I began to get into the spirit of things I became more and more animated in my speech. My voice rose up along with the strength of the message and the congregation reinforced me over and over again. At one point somebody shouted out, "Preach it, brother!"

Finally, after twenty minutes or so I brought my remarks to a close and sang, in Hebrew, the words of the benediction I used to conclude services in the synagogue. Then I offered a translation. "May God bless you and keep you. May God cause the light of the divine presence to shine on you and grace you. May God lift the divine presence up to you and grant you the blessing of inner peace. May this be God's desire. Amen."

The people again filled the room with Amens, and the organist played a brief melody. And then Rev. McEachern was by my side. He whispered to me, "Are you okay." And I said, "I think so." He wrapped his arm around my shoulders and said to the congregation in a loud voice, "The boy can preach!" It was the best compliment I'd ever received.

Adventure to Auckland

After working and serving a series of congregations as rabbi, cantor, and educator for more than thirty-five years in diverse places—Memphis, Tennessee; Sacramento, California; Youngstown, Ohio; Dunedin, Florida; Greenville, North Carolina; each for just a few years followed by Lincoln, Nebraska for many years—I was fortunate enough to be offered the chance to work in New Zealand for three years.

The year was 2001. I was very pleased to pursue this opportunity since I was pretty sure I was nearing the final stages of my professional life, and I thought it would be wonderful to spend a few years working in the beautiful island nation. Once I finalized the visa requirements I flew there for an interview that was a follow up to the Skype interview I'd had a few weeks before. I liked the people I'd met electronically, and apparently they liked me as well, enough for them to invite me to come for an in-person interview. I remember being a little apprehensive about the flight. I would depart from Los Angeles and be in the air for seventeen hours over the Pacific Ocean. I never thought I'd be in an airplane for such a long time, but it wasn't too bad. I had a business-class seat and I was able to sleep pretty well for part of the journey.

When I finally arrived in Auckland I was met at the airport by a couple members of the community. They drove me to a hotel, told me to get some rest, and informed me I'd be going out to dinner that evening with some of the members of the rabbinic search committee. The next four or five days are a busy blur in my memory. I met with the ritual committee, the education committee, the officers of

Adventure to Auckland

the board of trustees, the board itself, and importantly (I thought), the synagogue's secretary. I could tell that she was the one who really ran things there and I knew that if I ended up working there for the upcoming three years, she would be the one who would guide me and help me to avoid the usually inevitable mistakes newcomers make.

A couple weeks after I returned to the United States I was offered the position. I was happy about that and began, almost frantically, to take care of all the many details involved in such a move, temporary though it might be. The hardest part of the process was getting a visa that would allow me to work. The bureaucracy in our country is difficult to deal with, and so is the bureaucracy in New Zealand, made all the more so by my lack of cultural knowledge of the place. But, after a time, everything was set to go.

It was in September of that year that the Twin Towers and the Pentagon were attacked by terrorists who had hijacked four airliners. One of them, known as flight 93, crashed at Shanksville, Pennsylvania, as its doomed passengers attempted to wrest control of it from the terrorists. It was a terrible and tragic day for our country, and America entered what could only be called a state of war. The world was in turmoil. America was in shock and enraged at the same time, and here I was about to head off for a place that seemed as if it would be an adventure in paradise. I thought about changing my plans and remaining in the United States for the duration, but in retrospect I'm glad I didn't do that. I anticipated that my time in New Zealand would be a fitting ending for my career of service to Jewish communities. I really believed I would retire once the three years I'd agreed to came to an end. I didn't end up actually doing that, but it was a nice thought.

I very much enjoyed my time in New Zealand. Auckland was a hustling and bustling big city. The traffic around town was intense and almost terrifying to a person like me who struggled to drive on what felt like the wrong side of the road. But I got used to that, and I also got used to the differences in the way the congregation

Mr. Levine and Me

functioned compared to what I was used to back in America. My time in New Zealand was filled with new experiences, new opportunities to learn about others, and additions to the circle of friends that I'd likely never see again once I returned to the United States. Some of those friends are part of the stories scattered among the pages of this book.

Honorary Māori

While I was a part of the community in Auckland I became friendly with a Māori man, Tipani, who was a member of the congregation. He was a large, cheerful person who possessed a deep sense of reverence. He was traditional and modern at the same time, reticent about some things and forthcoming about others, as were many of the Māori people I met during my time there. He had a very peaceful demeanor, and was well liked by, I think, everyone. He had converted to Judaism some years before and was completely comfortable with his dual identity. I think he was, in many ways, a great asset to the community, serving on various committees and bringing some elements of Māori culture to the community.

One day when he and I were talking, Tipani invited me to come to the eighth-grade graduation of his niece, Hahana. It was to be held on a grassy area at the rear of a school for Māori kids not too far from the synagogue. On the afternoon of this event I rode with Tipani in his car. When we arrived I saw about two dozen little groups of people standing a short distance from a stage that had been set up on the grass. Each of these groups, Tipani told me, were the families of one of the children who were about to graduate eighth grade and move on to the next stages of their education. Tipani and I joined one of the groups. We all put our foreheads together, with our noses touching in Māori fashion. I had already learned this intimate form of greeting. The touching of noses was meant, in part, to allow those who were greeting one another to jointly breathe the same air and to become, in some way, one. I think it's so much better and so much more meaningful than a handshake.

After we had been there for maybe half an hour, a group of elders who were associated with the school and who I thought may have

Mr. Levine and Me

been tribal leaders, ascended the stage. Everyone in each of the assembled groups of families fell silent and turned to face the stage. A solemn sounding chant arose from the stage and was joined by the voices of the families. Following that, one of the elders made some remarks about the achievements of the children who were about to be recognized as graduates. Then another of the elders spoke about how this early education was the foundation for further education. A third person stood and held up a sheath of papers and began the graduation process.

It was a very interesting moment for me. I'd never witnessed such a personal sort of graduation. I'd attended many such events back in America. They were all pretty much the same: speeches by dignitaries and then a line of students crossing a stage to receive a certificate or diploma and a handshake. Usually someone took a photo of each student to be sold to their families at a later time. And then it would be over. That was not the way it was here in Auckland at this Māori school.

Each student was treated as an individual, an individual with the full support of a family group. As each student's name was called, some in English and others in traditional Māori, he or she came forward with their accompanying family group. The child spoke some words in Māori and then sang with their families. Tipani told me that each had a family song, and that is what each familial group was singing. The melodies were simple but lovely as they floated in the air above that grassy field.

After a time Tipani's niece was called, and as the family began to move forward toward the stage, I hung back since I was just a visitor. But Tipani reached out and grabbed me at the elbow. "Come with us, rabbi," he said. I said that this was for family, but he insisted. "Come and sing with us." I responded that I didn't know the melody or the Māori words. He smiled and said, "You're a great singer. You can follow along. Make up a harmony part. And don't worry about the words. You can just sing *la, la, la.*"

Adventure to Auckland

He kept his big hand on my arm as we approached the stage, almost as if he thought I might bolt and run away from what he had asked me to do. When the family began to sing its song I joined in with them as best I could. Tipani was singing in full voice beside me and my *la la la* was pretty much drowned out. When the song was completed his niece went up on the stage to receive her certificate. Noses were pressed, the elders were smiling, and she came back to her family group with a happy glow upon her face.

When the last of the family groups completed this beautiful ritual, steam tables I hadn't noticed before were opened and everyone formed a line to get a plate of traditional foods. Kumara (a kind of sweet potato), fish, shredded roast lamb, a dessert of corn pudding and many other items were all on the menu, and quite delicious. We spent a couple hours eating and socializing. The families mingled and enjoyed each other, and the children ran about as children do. There was a lot of nose-pressing, too. Nobody seemed to notice that I was one of the few non-Māori people there. I felt completely accepted.

On the way back to the car Tipani told me I had taken part in a very important moment in the life of part of his family. I told him I had enjoyed being there and how nice it had been to be so warmly welcomed. Then he told me something that surprised me. He said that I had sung the family song, and I made a crack about how skilled I was with the Māori language. He laughed and said that *la, la, la* was universal. And then he said again, "You have sung the family song." "That means you are part of the family," he continued. "*Nau mai*! Welcome!"

I felt a deep sense of honor as Tipani said those words to me. I didn't know how to respond so I remained silent, and so did he for a while. After a long silence he laughed a long, loud, deep laugh, and then he said, still smiling, "You should hope that nothing ever happens to Hahana's family. If it does you will have a new daughter."

I'm happy when I remember how a Jewish Māori let me become a Māori Jew.

It Is a Goat Leg

In certain neighborhoods in Aukland, streets run along the crests of some pretty steep hills. When the city was young, homes had been built along those streets, but as the population grew and the need for places to build homes grew as well, someone had the smart idea of building homes down the hill behind the original ones. I lived in a rented house that was three down from the street corner. There was another house further down the hill behind where I was living. All four of these houses shared a common driveway. It was a good system, a good use of the available land.

Sometimes I would go up to the street for a walk or for a bit of cycling. I had to walk my bicycle up the drive because it was so steep. One day while I was out for a walk I met a young man and woman who were also out for a walk. He was quite a handsome young man, short and dark skinned with neatly trimmed jet-black hair and beard. His wife was very pretty, also short, and as perfect as a doll. She was so very pregnant that I wondered how she could possibly navigate the hilly streets. We stood there and spoke for a little while and I learned their names. His was Rehan and hers was Harshini. They were beautiful names that meant "sunrise" or "dawn and joy," respectively. I also learned they lived at the end of the street, in the second house down the driveway. The baby Harshini was carrying was due very soon and she and Rehan were very excited about that. Harshini told me that her mother and father would be arriving from Sri Lanka the next day and would stay with them until she became skilled at motherhood.

It Is a Goat Leg

A few days later when I was out walking, Rehan came running up the street toward me. As he came closer he shouted, "We have a baby girl, we have a baby girl!" He was so excited. Down the hill there was an older couple, obviously his relatives. The man was short and stout and very dignified looking, with graying hair and beard, and skin as dark as ebony. The woman looked like an older version of Harshini, slim and very lovely, with long, flowing hair. She was dressed in what I thought must be traditional garb, a beautiful, printed sari with a knitted blue sash around her waist. They were a handsome couple. Rehan introduced them to me as Harshini's parents and we shook hands and slightly bowed to one another. Then Rehan told me there would be a gathering at their home in two days' time and that I should come and be with them to celebrate the birth of their daughter. I said that I would be there and Rehan said, as he walked away with his in-laws, "You will be glad you did. Harshini's mother is the best cook in the world!"

At the appointed time I went to Rehan's and Harshini's home. Harshini's mother had created a feast of traditional Sri Lankan finger foods and there were trays of samosas, fried lentil doughnuts, fish patties, bowls of yellow rice, and sweets like chocolate fingers. I tried a little bit of everything during a very happy social time with a houseful of strangers. It was all very delicious and matched up well with the friendliness exhibited by everyone there.

After an hour or so I decided it was time to leave, and I found Rehan and Harshini and wished them well. They smiled and wished me well in return, thanked me for being with them, and walked me to the door. I walked up the driveway to the street and then began trudging up the hill toward my home. Before I went too far Rehan came out to the street and called out, "Michael, Michael, wait." He trotted up the hill carrying a bag. He was followed by his father-in-law. When he reached me he handed me the bag and told me it was a gift from Harshini and himself. I thanked him and noticed the bag was ice cold. So I asked what it was. He was smiling as he looked at me and said, "It is a goat leg."

Mr. Levine and Me

His father-in-law had reached us by then, just as I said, "No one has ever given me a goat leg before." At that moment, his father-in-law looked at me and smiled. "In our village," he said, "if someone gives you a goat leg it means you are a part of the family." I was touched and honored.

When I got home I got online to look for goat leg recipes. I found one that looked good to me, Jamaican jerk roast goat leg. Once the goat leg was defrosted a couple of days later, I roasted it and carried it down the hill to my new friends' home. I told everyone that I had roasted the goat leg and that I'd like to share it with them. Harshini's mother quickly set the table and brought out a couple of trays of leftover finger foods from the celebration a few days before, and we sat down to share a meal together. As a family.

An Indonesian Chanukah

I had been living and working in New Zealand for a couple of years when the governments of Australia and Indonesia organized what was called a World Peace Forum. The theme of the forum, announced as the first in a series, was to be centered on interfaith cooperation as an antidote to terrorism. Many Pacific nations, New Zealand among them, were invited to send delegations, and the process began to select members of the delegation from each country's various ethnic and religious communities.

About a year prior to this I had been invited to give a sermon, coincidentally on the subject of interfaith cooperation, by the pastor of a large Anglican Church in Aukland. I believe he was also the Anglican Bishop of Aukland. On the day I gave that sermon, the Prime Minister, Helen Clark, was in the congregation. Following the service I had a chance to say hello and shake hands with her. I don't know if that had anything to do with my being selected to be the Jewish member of the New Zealand delegation a year later, but somehow I was chosen for that role. It seemed a little strange to me at the time since I was not a citizen. Someone who had been at the meeting at which the delegation was put together told me that when my name was proposed, someone mentioned my non-citizen status and someone else said something like, "We're a small country. He can be an honorary Kiwi for this conference." However it happened, I became a representative of New Zealand and its Jewish community at the 2004 World Peace Forum. Since the forum was to take place in Indonesia, I saw it as a wonderful opportunity to visit a place I would never otherwise have had a chance of seeing.

In December of 2004, I boarded a plane for Indonesia with a good-sized group of New Zealanders of every faith and ethnic background represented in the country. We flew from Auckland to Perth and then to Jakarta. After a night in an airport hotel I boarded another plane that took me to Yogyakarta in Central Java. I had been selected to deliver one of the addresses during the conference and my preparation for that was complete, so I planned to just enjoy whatever activities had been planned. Since the holiday of Chanukah would begin two days after we arrived in Yogyakarta I'd brought along a menorah and candles so I'd be able to share the Chanukah experience with anyone who might be interested.

On the second day of the gathering I made my speech, and while I was speaking I noticed that among the dignitaries seated in the front row was the President of Indonesia, Susilo Bambang Yudhoyono. He was a large, imposing man, with a military bearing. I knew him because I had seen photographs of him at the airport in Jakarta and also on some billboards in Yogyakarta. I hoped I would get to meet him. Following my speech and a time for questions and answers he and his entourage approached me and we all shook hands. The president thanked me for being a part of the program. Then they turned and filed out of the room.

The next few days were filled with meetings and workshops, brainstorming sessions, and good food and time for socializing. The fact that this was all happening in Indonesia didn't stop me from thinking that the conference was not very different from the many conferences I'd attended over the years in the United States. Lots of good people getting together to try and deal with the problems of the world followed, I think, the same protocols no matter where in the world such gatherings took place.

During the afternoon of the day that would end with the start of Chanukah, I spoke with someone from the hotel staff and one of the conference staff people and explained that I would like to extend an invitation to everyone to join me in the traditional lighting of the menorah that evening. Arrangements were made right there to reserve a space near the hotel lobby for this to take place. I told them I'd need a small table for the menorah and mentioned that

It Is a Goat Leg

back home there would be some kind of fried food to commemorate the miracle of the oil in the Chanukah story. Latkes or doughnuts, for example. I spent another few minutes going over the story of the holiday and was assured that the place would be ready and that all the delegates would be notified. When I returned to my room after the last session of the day, I found an invitation that had been slipped under the door. It was for the celebration of Chanukah that would take place near the lobby at seven thirty.

I got the menorah from its box, put a couple of candles in my pocket, and went to the space near the lobby at a little after seven. I set up the menorah and waited with a bit of anticipation for people to arrive. The time moves slowly when you are waiting for something. After about ten or fifteen minutes I began to feel a little angst. I was the only person there. Just me and my menorah. Another ten minutes went by. Still no one had arrived. *So much for interfaith unity*, I thought, just as a hotel employee in his red uniform came into the space. He knew who I was somehow and said, "Rabbi, we are so sorry—we had to move your event to another space." He picked up the little table with its menorah and told me to follow him. We went down a corridor and he stopped and opened a door for me. I went into the room and it was filled with people waiting for me to arrive. There were perhaps a half dozen Jewish delegates in total from New Zealand, Hong Kong, and Australia, and about three hundred others from a multitude of backgrounds. I think that virtually every one of the delegates was there. I went to the microphone, told a bit of the story of the Maccabees, and explained the legend of the one-day supply of oil for the ancient Temple's menorah that miraculously lasted for eight days. Then I lit the first candle and used it to light the other as I sang the traditional Chanukah blessings.

The lights, which had been dimmed, came up and everyone was smiling. A round of applause echoed through the room just as two doors at the rear of the room opened and several waiters entered carrying trays of, you guessed it, fried doughnuts.

It was the best first night of Chanukah I can remember.

Why Are You Laughing

The World Peace Forum in Yogyakarta came to a close and I tried to say goodbye to some of the people I had met as they waited for their airport transportation. I was going to stay in Indonesia another few days and had arranged to tour the sights with a young man, Ismail, who worked for the hotel and had a side business taking tourists around in his Ford Explorer.

The following day we left the hotel very early and drove to several nearby places my guide thought might be of interest to me. He brought me to a place where beautiful batik dyed fabrics were created, and I bought some for gifts. One of those I bought gifts for was Harshini, my neighbor in Auckland whose husband had gifted me with a goat leg. Another piece of batik fabric was for the synagogue's secretary, Christine. I got a few other things for some people in the United States that I would bring to them the next time I returned there. We spent the rest of the morning going in and out of little shops in very crowded neighborhoods whose streets were filled with multitudes of motor scooters darting in and out between the cars and trucks. There were many tourists going into shops along those crowded streets. It reminded me of the way Times Square used to be in the bad old days.

In the middle of the day I told my driver, who I now thought of as my young friend Ismail, that I thought it was time to stop and get something to eat. He said we were not near the hotels and I told him I didn't want to eat at a hotel but at some place where he would like to eat. I was in Java and wanted to eat like a Javanese person would. He smiled and took off down the road at a pretty fast

Why Are You Laughing

clip. We wound through tiny streets, turning left and right a good number of times until he stopped on a street filled with more little shops with wooden awnings propped up over the walkway. When we walked over toward one of these shops the aroma of something delicious enveloped us and I could feel a pang of anticipation for a good lunch.

Behind the counter of the little shop with the wooden awning there was a young woman. She wore an apron and had what my grandmother would have called a babushka on her head. I turned to Ismail and asked him to order for us, but he declined and said that I should pick out the foods we would eat for lunch. There was an array of delectable looking finger foods on trays behind the counter. So I pointed and said, "Two of those, and two of those, and two of those..." until I had selected enough for both of us. As I was pointing, the young woman began to laugh. And she continued to laugh each time I pointed out one of the items to be put on our paper plates. I asked her why she was laughing, and she just laughed some more. Finally I asked Ismail why she was laughing, so he approached the counter and asked her something in one of the Indonesian languages. Then he started to laugh also. So I said to him, "Why are you laughing now?" And he said, "She told me you are the very first foreigner who has ever stopped here to eat her food. She loves you very much for that." I smiled at the young woman behind the counter. I'm not sure, but I think she blushed.

Ismail and I sat down on a bench beside a large tree and ate the wonderful foods, foods that were made even more wonderful by the laughter of the young woman behind the counter.

I loved her very much for her laughter and her love. And her food!

What is it Like to Live in a Muslim Country?

The day after my encounter with the local food, Ismail took me to two very famous places, both of them not far from the hotel in Yogyakarta. The first was Prambanan, a Hindu temple compound built in the ninth century. Much of it has deteriorated over time but quite of bit of restoration has been done. Even in its diminished state it is an amazing place.

After spending a few hours there Ismail said we should leave so that I would have time to see another wonderful place, the ancient Buddhist temple Borobudur. We parked quite a distance from the temple, which dominated the skyline. It was enormous. The temple rises to ten stories, with stairways and walkways all around its outer part. On the walls, according to the plaque I read, there are fourteen hundred carved stone panels depicting the life of the Buddha and some Indigenous Javan themes as well. The temple was built in the eighth century and was abandoned sometime in the fourteenth century as the Hindu kingdoms in Indonesia went into decline. There have been a couple restorations of the temple. Ismail told me that in the 1980s a restoration was needed because of the destruction caused by an earthquake. This was done by the Indonesian government and UNESCO, and great pains had been taken to reuse the original materials. The temple is the largest Buddhist shrine in the world and is still the focus of pilgrimages. It's listed as a UNESCO World Heritage Site.

What is it Like to Live in a Muslim Country?

Ismail and I walked toward this magnificent structure across the large grassy park that surrounded it. There were lots of tourists roaming around and a small army of souvenir vendors approaching everyone trying to sell whatever they had on offer. I waved off a number of these vendors but when I got near the stairway that was the entrance to the temple I said to two young women vendors that I would buy something on the way out. One of them said, "You remember us. We will remember you." Ismail and I followed the path of pilgrims, stopping to look at many of the carvings. He explained some of them to me, and others were easily understood. When we got to the top after an hour or so, I was amazed to see a multitude of bell-shaped structures made of stone. Each of them had a sort of window and Ismail told me that pilgrims would look into each of them until they saw a statue of the Buddha inside. There was also a massive head of the Buddha on that top level, gazing out at the countryside beyond. I was amazed at the scope of this place and in awe of the efforts that had to have gone into building it so many centuries ago. The placed reeked of a spiritual energy that was palpable.

We took another hour coming back down from the top of the Temple and the final long stairway, and then we were back in the park. We started walking toward where the Ford Explorer was parked and just a few minutes passed before we heard a voice calling out, "You remember us. We remember you." It was, of course, the two young vendors I had promised to buy something from. They came up to us, smiling and happy, and opened their cases to display their wares. I selected a few things to purchase from each of them. They thanked me and we stood there in the park and talked for a little while. Soon it seemed as if we knew each other, not as sellers and buyer, but as people who certainly could be friends. I liked these two people just as I had come to like my young friend Ismail.

At some point, feeling comfortable enough to do so, I asked what it was like to live in a Muslim country. Both of these women looked at me with a quizzical expression on their faces. Then one of them

Mr. Levine and Me

said, "We don't live in a Muslim country." I said something about Indonesia being a large country with almost two hundred million people, eighty percent of whom were Muslim. I think these two young women realized that I had no agenda and was just asking because I honestly wished to know. One of the young women cleared up all my questions when she said, "We don't live in a Muslim country. We live in a country where many Muslims live." They drew near and both of them hugged me warmly.

Ismail took a photo of that hug with my camera, which he was holding for me. When I returned to New Zealand I had the film in that camera developed and then, to my surprise, there were the two young Indonesian vendors, hugging me as if I were a beloved relative. I cherish that photograph to this day. And it got me to think about my own country. I now knew the answer I would give if someone asked me, "What is it like to live in a Christian country?" I would say, "I don't live in a Christian country. I live in a country where many Christians live."

A New Call to Service

When I finished my work in New Zealand and returned to the United States, I thought for a while about trying to start a retreat center somewhere and live out my years meditating and teaching. I thought about a little village in Oaxaca, Mexico, but that didn't work out (more on this later).

After a while I decided to settle down back in Lincoln, Nebraska, where I had spent so many years. I was able to buy a modest house on a pleasant street in a quiet neighborhood. I worked a lot on a landscape plan. It was good to be digging in the dirt, planting, and mulching. As little by little I got the house up to par it began to feel like home. I was comfortable there and in a few months I began to feel like a retired person. It was hard for me to get used to not going to work every day, to be a man without a schedule, but after a time it began to feel normal. Cooking, gardening, meditation group in the basement once a week, a little writing, family dinners and occasional attendance at the synagogue where I had served for many years became routine for me. It was a nice life, a pleasant retirement.

One Sunday afternoon I got a call out of the blue from the president of a synagogue in Queens, New York. She said my name had been recommended to her congregation. She told me her synagogue was seeking a rabbi who would be willing to come and serve for a few years and help get them on track. I remember her saying the congregation felt like a rudderless ship at the moment and it was in need of a steady hand. In that initial call she invited me to come to New York for an interview. I told her I had retired a couple years earlier and would have to think about it.

When we hung up I thought that was the end of it, but a couple weeks later the same person called and asked me again to come to

Mr. Levine and Me

New York for an interview. It's funny how nice it felt to be pursued like this. So I said that maybe it would be best to set up a phone interview to see if we all at least liked each other. If that worked out okay, I said, then maybe we could schedule a visit. She agreed and we set up a time the next weekend for the phone call.

The interview call came on a Sunday afternoon. After pleasantries were exchanged, people on the other end of the conference call asked a few pretty mundane questions, which I answered as best I could, and after about half an hour someone said they knew enough about me and offered me the position that was open. It sounded to me that the congregation was pretty desperate to find a rabbi, and I wondered what the trouble was there. So I said I couldn't make that decision just then and suggested that we schedule a visit so that I could learn more about their community and congregation and decide whether or not I thought it would be a good fit.

I made the trip to New York a couple weeks later and pretty much interviewed the people who were supposed to be interviewing me. It was obviously a congregation in decline, and I knew it was either going to find some leadership or continue its downward slide. I've always liked a challenge, and this was certainly one of those. After a couple of days I agreed to come and serve as rabbi of the congregation, with the stipulation that it would be for just a few years. I hoped I'd be able to lead the community to a better place and then turn things over to someone else. One of the things that helped me to decide was the fact that this synagogue was the very one in which my ordination ceremony had taken place years before. It was like time had circled around from the end and returned me to the beginning.

Before it was over, the two or so years I had agreed to had grown to eight years of service at the temple in New York. I think I left that community better than I found it when I finally retired and returned to my home in Lincoln. I had also seen a few new adventures along the way.

You Are Weisser

At just about the middle of my time in Queens I got a call from the office of the Consul General of Indonesia. The person I spoke with told me that the consul general would like to meet with me and share a cup of tea. "Are you free tomorrow?" she asked. I looked at my calendar and said that I was free anytime the next day. The person who called said they would be happy to send a car for me at eleven the next morning, and I was glad to hear that. Without that the trip to the consulate building would involve taking the 7 train from Flushing to Times Square, then the A or D train uptown to Columbus Circle, then a crosstown bus to the East Side, and then a bit of a walk to the consulate. I asked why the consul general wanted to meet with me and the person who had called told me she didn't know.

The next day the car arrived, and I got over to Manhattan the easy way. The driver let me sit in front and we chatted along the way. As we pulled up in front of the consulate on East 68th Street, the driver got out, opened the door for me, and walked me to the entrance of the consulate. I think that is the only time I've ever experienced something like that, being treated like some kind of big shot. The driver told me he would take me back to Queens when I was finished inside. I thanked him and entered the building.

There were about twenty-five people in the entry area. Waiters were walking around with trays of various foods and plates to serve them on. Others were busy pouring tea. Everyone was in dresses or suits. I was glad I had thought to wear a suit and tie that day. I often

Mr. Levine and Me

wore jeans and a short-sleeved shirt when working in my office at the synagogue.

After about half an hour we were all invited to a room that had been set up with chairs. There was a screen at the front of the room with a film of a Balinese opera playing. The dancers in the film were wearing long, colorful, flowing garments and had carved masks covering their faces. The music and the people singing were a little familiar to me, with clanging gongs and loud drumbeats and discordant melodies. I realized it seemed familiar because it was something I had experienced before back in 2004, at the conclusion of a conference I attended in Indonesia. I recalled lighting the Chanukah menorah with all the other delegates from around the Pacific Rim, my Indonesian first night of Chanukah, before heading off for the closing dinner of the conference at the palace of the Sultan of Yogyakarta. The entertainment that evening was a performance of Balinese opera very much like what I was seeing on the screen before me at the consulate.

I was enjoying the performance when it suddenly stopped and a very handsome middle-aged woman came to the lectern. It was the consul general. She welcomed us and introduced a speaker who went on about the need for interfaith cooperation in the world and proclaimed that Indonesia was a leader in this effort.

When the presentation was over, the consul general thanked everyone for being there and then left the room. I was a little confused because I thought I was supposed to have an appointment with her. I picked up a few brochures from one of the tables and began to make my way to the exit when someone on the consulate staff came over to me and said, "Please come with me. The consul general will see you now." He escorted me to an office and introduced me to the consul general, saying "This is Rabbi Weisser from Queens" (I don't know how he knew my name. I'd never seen him before). He bowed slightly and left the room.

The consul general sat down on a couch and invited me to join her. She asked if I would like some tea and I said I would and thanked

You Are Weisser

her. Then she said, "You were at the first World Peace Forum in Yogyakarta, and we would like it very much if you would attend the fourth World Peace Forum. It will be held in Bogor, which is also in Java." I said I would need to check my calendar and arrange for the time to be away from my responsibilities. She told me they would need to know in the next couple of days so that the consulate could arrange for a visa, plane tickets, and accommodations in Indonesia. I told her I'd have the answer the same afternoon and would call her. She then told me that if I were able to attend she'd send the driver out to pick up my passport so that she could get my visa taken care of. Before I left she handed me a gift-wrapped box and told me she hoped I would enjoy what was inside.

When I got back to my office, I cleared my calendar for the dates of the conference, let the synagogue leadership know that I would be away to a conference in Indonesia, and called the consulate to let them know I was able to attend. Then I opened the package I had received from the consul general. It was a beautiful batik shirt. I would take it with me to the conference and wear it to the more formal events, which I remembered always had a dress code calling for "Long Sleeves/Religious/Batik."

The next morning the driver arrived to pick up my passport and about a week later brought it back to me, along with airline tickets and a reservation card for the hotel in Bogor. I wondered how the consul general had known I was in Queens, but I didn't dwell on it. It was odd though.

I arrived in Bogor on the twenty-second of November. It was 2012, almost eight years after my first visit to that country, when I had been an improbable representative of New Zealand. The conference was very much like the earlier one. There were speakers on various topics, workshops, brainstorming sessions, good food and times for socializing. I ran into a few people I'd met nearly eight years before in Yogyakarta and generally had a good time. I was not a scheduled speaker this time but I did participate in a couple of the Q & A sessions.

Mr. Levine and Me

The last evening of the event we were reminded that the next day we'd be bused to a place for a meeting and photo op with the president. Susilo Bambang Yudhoyono still held that office, having been elected to a second term a couple years before. When we got to the venue, a beautiful old Dutch colonial government building, we all took our seats. President Yudhoyono came in and made a few remarks to thank us all for being there, and then the process of taking individual photos began. It was exactly the way it had been in 2004. When it was my turn I walked to the front, shook hands with the president, and waited for the picture to be taken. The president looked at me and said, "I think I know you." And I replied that I knew him, but I was sure he didn't know me. Then he said, "Where do I know you from?" I thought for a few seconds and said, "Yogyakarta, 2004." He looked at me and smiled. Then he said, still smiling, "You are Weisser."

I was blown away. I couldn't believe this man, president of a very large country, had recalled my name, pulled it from the thousands of names of people he met in the course of any year. But he had. I have trouble pronouncing his name even if it is printed before my eyes. He got mine just right. It was a humbling moment.

Sometimes There is No Good Answer

For a guy who has not always been overtly religious, it seems a little odd to me that there have been a number of rabbis and other clergy who have been influential at key moments in my life. Every so often one of them popped up and passed along some bit of wisdom to me. The first one I remember is Andrew Klein. He was the rabbi of Temple Keser Israel in New Haven, Connecticut. He was short and solid looking, with a stern appearance. He spoke with a slight Germanic accent. He had gray close-cropped hair and a mustache. He was very dignified looking, always wearing a suit and tie and a black yarmulka.

When I was a very young child living on Uncle Nick's chicken farm, my family became members of the West Shore Jewish Community Center. This was a makeshift synagogue that met in a space that was rented from the Grange, a farmers' organization, in Branford, Connecticut. We went there for Sunday school each week during the school year. While the children were learning about holidays and basic Jewish ideas, the parents would either be studying a bit of Torah or drinking coffee and schmoozing as they waited for the children to be finished. Most weeks the teachers taught about the terrible events of the Holocaust and the establishment of the State of Israel. They taught this over and over, about the Holocaust and the miracle of the Jewish State. It was always the Holocaust and Israel, Israel and the Holocaust (it almost seemed that we were being taught that there was some connection between the two things). The impression I had, even at the age of about eight years, was that the Jewish People were able to establish Israel as a sort of reward for having endured the terrors of the Holocaust. I was bothered, then and now, by that idea.

About once a month Rabbi Klein would come out from New Haven and conduct a class for the adults and follow that with a brief service for everyone. Following the service there were always refreshments, cookies and juice usually, and all the kids would sit on the floor with the adults sitting on folding chairs or standing around them as the rabbi asked if anybody had any questions of Jewish interest. One week I raised my hand and the rabbi invited me to ask my question. So I stood up and said something like, "We've been learning about the Holocaust and that six million Jews and five million other people were murdered in the Holocaust by the Nazis. We also learned we now have a Jewish country somehow as a result of all that terrible suffering. So Rabbi, I want to ask you, is the State of Israel worth eleven million dead people?" Some people might think I was precocious.

There was an immediate uproar in the room. Parents, my own included, shouted at me, "How dare you ask the rabbi something like that?" People seemed genuinely offended that I had done that. Rabbi Klein held up his hand and quieted everyone down. And he said to me, "Michael, that is a very good question. And I have to tell you I don't have a good answer for you. Sometimes there is no good answer." And then, speaking to the parents, he said, "We should all think long and hard about Michael's question."

From that day to this I have thought of Rabbi Klein as a decent, honest teacher who was strong enough to acknowledge that he didn't have all the answers. I don't know what answer I was expecting when I asked Rabbi Klein that question so long ago. I do know, though, that sometimes "I don't know" is the best answer of all.

I'm Teaching Him Because...

If you come into my kitchen you will find an organized space. I know where everything is. I always put things away in the same place. There are never dishes in the sink. Pots and pans and casserole dishes are clean and ready for their next use. I keep some of my favorite recipes in a little decorated metal index-card box that lives on the top of the back of my stove. It's been in that place of honor for many years, atop whichever stove I happened to have in whichever home I've lived in over the years. My pantry is organized in such a way that I never have to search for an ingredient. I add things to a shopping list when those things are running low. I know how to use my appliances and kitchen tools. My kitchen is like that because my grandmother Sophie taught me long ago that it is supposed to be that way. Every time I take my chef's knife out of its sheath I remember my grandmother Sophie. She is the one who first taught me how to use a chef's knife. I was no more than ten years old when she taught me to do that. It's a skill that has served me well over the years I've been cooking.

I'm pretty sure I love to be in the kitchen putting together a batch of holubtsi or kielbasa kapusta, or baking challah or Jewish rye bread, because when I'm doing such things I feel like I'm bringing my grandmother Sophie back to life, that somehow she is there with me reminding me to go easy on the salt. Some of the things I like to cook come directly from Bubbe Sofia, and many other things I like

Mr. Levine and Me

to prepare are not from her, like my Italian dishes. But everything I cook is somehow bound up with her because it was she who got me started with my love of the kitchen and the wonders that happen there.

About four years ago, when my grandson Isaac was about eight years old, the family got together to eat spaghetti and meatballs at my home. I had made a pot of my marinara sauce, a big batch of meatballs, spaghetti, and a nice green salad. (*I mustn't forget the Italian cheesecake I made for dessert that day.*) The chef's knife played a big part in that meal, like all the meals I so enjoy cooking.

We were all seated around my dining room table: my son David and his wife, Jenny, and their three kids—Elise, Marin, and Isaac—and my daughter Dina and her husband, Chris, and their two kids—Lilyana and Noah. We recited a traditional blessing before we began to eat, and then plates were filled and everyone began to dig in.

Well, my grandson Noah was in his "I won't eat anything but a hot dog stage" at the time, so that meant there were a few extra meatballs for somebody else around the table. Isaac had a few meatballs on his plate and at some point he leaned over to his mom, who was seated next to him, and we all heard him say to her, "If they had a meatball-eating contest with grandpa's meatballs, I would win!" People laughed about that, and everyone kept eating. It was a lovely moment for me. From that day forward Isaac was known as the Meatball King, a title he proudly wore.

Sometime later, I took a break from my writing to go across the road to my mailbox. There was a card from Isaac among the pile of junk mail. I figured it was probably a thank you note for the present I'd sent to him for his twelfth birthday a couple weeks before. When I got back into the house I opened Isaac's card and found a message that brought on a smile and a pretty good chuckle. It was a thank-you note. I was glad Jenny and David were raising him right. His note read, "Dear Grandpa Michael, Thanks so much for the $50. I'm buying a new bike and that makes it easier. And I'm so outraged that the post office won't let you send meatballs. Love, Isaac."

I'm Teaching Him Because...

But back to Bubbe Sofia and the chef's knife. I was ten years old learning how to roll a chef's knife as I chopped ribs of celery in my grandmother's kitchen. She taught me how to hold the knife, how to tuck in my fingers so I wouldn't chop them instead of the celery, and how to get such prep chores done quickly and easily. *[She didn't yet let me peel potatoes with a paring knife because one time when I tried to do that she said she had to go back and peel the peels when I was done.]* Anyway, I was happily chopping celery that my grandmother was going to use for a pot of soup she was about to put together when my mother came into the kitchen. This was in about 1951, an era when gender roles were pretty standardized for boys and girls. Boys learned to build things and girls learned to cook and clean. That's just the way it was in those days.

So, my mother said to my grandmother, "Why are you teaching him that? He's a boy." And my grandmother, without missing a beat, responded to my mother, her daughter, "I'm teaching him so he'll never have to depend on someone like you." My mother shrugged and left the room. Every time I'm cooking something that memory comes to mind. My grandmother had given me a great gift, one that has served me well.

An old portrait photo of Bubbe Sofia has hung in a prominent place in my kitchen for much of my adult life. Sometimes I sense her presence and just know she's there to guide my hand so that I won't cut myself as I chop the celery.

They'll Never Know

When I was growing up around Legion Avenue in New Haven things were pretty difficult for my family. There was never any money. We never owned a car. We were among the last people to get a television set.

My brother and I were always looking for ways to make a couple of bucks. It was the same for many of the other families in the neighborhood. I remember pumping gas sometimes at Mr. Michael's Esso station after school when I was in the ninth or tenth grade. There was no such thing as self-serve then and I'd pump the gasoline, clean the windshield, and check the oil. Mr. Michael told us kids who pumped gas for him to always remember to tell customers that they needed a generator belt or a radiator hose. "Remember," he'd say, "Everybody needs a belt or hose." If we got someone to buy one we would get a little bonus. For a while I had two paper routes, one in the morning and one in the afternoon. As you've read in earlier episodes in this book, I swept the floor of a bakery after school for a while and the owner, Mr. Levine, gave me a quarter each day for my trouble.

I had another means of earning money in those days, at least for a little while. I knew something about the kosher rules from my Sunday school classes at the synagogue. I knew, for example, which animals could be kosher. Only those with cloven hooves that also chewed their cud. That eliminated pigs; they had cloven hooves, but they didn't chew their cud. The same for camels; they chewed their cud but didn't have cloven hooves. All of that was spelled out in the Torah and the Bible. As for birds, only the birds that were not birds of prey were acceptable. There was also an obscure rule that any animal or bird that happened to die of its own accord could not be considered kosher. So roadkill was not okay. In order to be kosher, animals not only had to fit the formula given in the Torah but also be slaughtered in a ritually appropriate way.

By means of this basic knowledge I thought I could get to work at the open-air kosher chicken market in the neighborhood. That would be great, I thought. The market used kids like me to help out and paid thirty-five cents an hour. To make almost three dollars for a Sunday's work would be like a dream come true. Between that and sweeping Mr. Levine's bakery and my paper routes, I could be the richest kid in the neighborhood.

There was a woman who worked at the chicken market. She's the one who told me I could work there on Sundays. I didn't know her real name, but I always thought of her as Brunhilda, a name I never said aloud (she probably wouldn't have liked that). I gave her this mental nickname because she was tall and strong, always with a stern expression on her face. She had a thick accent like my grandfather Frank, or as he preferred, Franc. She was the kind of tough woman I'd seen in war movies during the Saturday matinee at the Whalley Theater, all business as she hurried me along. The other person at the chicken market was the *shochet*, or ritual slaughterer. He was a small man, an orthodox rabbi I think, who always sharpened his knife before he slit the throat of each chicken that needed killing. He always wore black pants, a white shirt speckled with red spots of blood, and an apron like a chef might wear, also covered with blood stains. Everyone called him Rav Aaron.

I was lucky enough for a few months one summer to help out at the chicken market. Every Sunday I'd go there and spend the day unloading crates of chickens from the back of a flatbed truck. I think there were six or eight chickens in each crate. Once I had a crate on the ground I had to reach in and pull out a live squawking bird and hand it over to Brunhilda. She would look it over and give it a quick inspection to be sure it was unblemished and uninjured. Either of those two things would render it not kosher. Once she was satisfied about the chicken she would hand it to the shochet, who would slice its throat with a smooth motion. Then he'd place it into a galvanized iron cone, head down, so that its blood could drain out into the gully in the cement below. When the chicken's blood stopped draining out someone from inside the building would take the chicken and remove its feathers. This was the routine every Sunday from ten in the morning until four in the afternoon. The last hour of the day was spent cleaning the place up. That chicken market was where I learned that things are not always what they seem to be.

There was another part of the Sunday routine. Before the day's work began Rav Aaron would take out his *t'fillin* [tefillin], those little boxes containing hand-calligraphed sections of the Torah, with their leather straps that pious Jews wrap around their arm and place on their foreheads during weekday prayers. He'd face the wall and quietly chant the words of the prayer service, bobbing and weaving in the traditional style known as *shukelling*. He'd stop the slaughtering process early in the afternoon for his afternoon prayers as well. Even though this kind of thing was foreign to me and my family and to all but the oldest members of the synagogue my family attended, I was impressed with Rav Aaron's dedication and devotion to the traditions he so openly embraced. I thought he was some kind of a holy man. I knew I would never be a follower of that brand of Judaism, but the vision of him praying in his very traditional way was with me anytime I went to the synagogue with my family.

One Sunday, as I was doing my job getting crates of chickens down from the truck and handing live chickens over to Brunhilda, I came across a chicken that had died in the crate. It had probably gotten suffocated by other chickens in the crowded crate. I handed it to Brunhilda and said, "This one's dead." She looked at it and said to the shochet, "Oy, we got a dead one." Rav Aaron snatched the dead chicken from her hands, ran his knife across its dead throat, placed it head down into the cone like every other chicken and said, "They'll never know."

They'll Never Know

I couldn't believe what I was seeing and hearing. All the reverence I had for this man, this pious shochet, this person who was scrupulous about reciting his prayers and keeping his knife sharp so as not to inflict an unnecessary pain on the chickens he was called upon to slaughter, that man was a fraud. I was as close to devastated as a fourteen-year-old could be.

I untied my rubber apron and threw it on the ground at Rav Aaron's feet. I glared at him. Then I turned to Brunhilda. She was untying her rubber apron. The stern look that was always on her face had become a look of disgust and anger. I don't know what she did next. I don't know what became of Rav Aaron either. I didn't ask for my thirty-five-cents-an-hour wage.

I never went back there again.

New York Deli Comes to the Prairie

The are only two viable Jewish communities in Nebraska. One in Lincoln, the capital city, and the other in Omaha, the state's largest city. There are three synagogues—Reform, Orthodox, and Conservative—and a Chabad house in Omaha; and two in Lincoln, Reform and Conservative, now semi-merged and sharing a joint religious school program for children, with one rabbi serving both. When I worked with the Reform synagogue in Lincoln it came to me that it might be a good idea to do some programming for the scattered little pockets of Jewish people who lived in parts of Nebraska that I called "outstate." I learned that some people who lived outstate didn't like that terminology much, so I mostly referred to them by other euphemisms, like "greater Nebraska." At any rate, I'd bring a program to them a couple times each year.

I had someone named Audrey, the chairperson of my education committee, helping me with this. Audrey had developed a mailing and email list so we could reach people in greater Nebraska and let them know a program would be taking place in one community or another. She also was a skilled grant writer and managed to get us some funding to help with these programs. Usually we were able to get a free space at one of the community colleges and things always worked out well. I loved bringing these programs out to the hinterlands, and I'm sure the people who came from far and wide to attend were glad to have an occasional connection with their heritage.

New York Deli Comes to the Prairie

Audrey and I were planning a program that would focus on the wonders of the Lower East Side of New York during the heyday of Jewish life there. The great waves of immigration in the late 1800s brought many different ethnicities and nationalities to America, including maybe a million Jewish Europeans and at least as many Italians. Jewish and Italian culture and customs became integral parts of the American experience in the Petri dish that was the Lower East Side. It didn't take very long for Jewish, Italian, and other immigrants to move on from the Lower East Side and populate neighborhoods all over the city and out on Long Island. One of the great contributions of the Italians was the creation of Italian American cuisine, something that all of us appreciate to this day. A great contribution of the Jewish immigrants was the kosher or kosher-style deli, places where gigantic, corned beef or pastrami sandwiches, barley mushroom soup and other delicacies could be had. Sadly, there are not too many of these left.

While I was talking with the members of the committee that was helping me with the program about the Lower East Side, someone suggested that we should have New York kosher-style deli for the luncheon during the program. What a great idea. But where in the world would be able to get New York deli in Nebraska. It seemed an impossible dream. But someone, I can't remember who, said they knew someone in Denver whose father ran a deli in New York City. His father was Barney Greengrass. That got my attention. Barney Greengrass - The Sturgeon King was my very favorite deli in New York. I'd been there a number of times during visits to the city. We got the phone number for the Denver son and someone from the committee made a call to him. When he learned what we were trying to do he said he'd speak with his father and see if we could make something happen. A few days later he called back and said that his father would help out any way he could. He gave us a phone number and when that call was finished we called Barney Greengrass, the Sturgeon King.

Mr. Levine and Me

We reached Barney Greengrass that day and after talking for a while he said he would send whatever we needed. He asked how many people would be involved, and I told him about sixty or so. Then he said he would put things up in cold boxes and FedEx them to me to arrive the day before the event. I couldn't believe our good fortune. He asked if anyone in Lincoln traveled to Chicago on business and I knew there were several people in the community who often did. He said it would be best if they got the bread there since the rye bread he used at the deli had a short shelf life. Better to have it fresh. He gave us the name and address of a bakery in Chicago and we were lucky enough to have someone who would be returning from there the day before our event. That person agreed to pick up the bread and bring it on the plane with him when he returned.

The day before the event three large cooler boxes were delivered to me at the synagogue and the bread connection turned up with a dozen beautiful loaves of pre-sliced Jewish rye with lots of caraway seeds. We were all set. I guess as an article of faith we had already announced to the greater Nebraska folks that the program was going to be called "Jewish Deli Comes to the Prairie." We never got a bill for the things we received from the Sturgeon King. There was a note in one of the coolers that let us know it was a gift to the synagogue.

The morning of the event, we loaded Audrey's van with everything Barney Greengrass's had sent, along with the bags of Jewish rye bread and all the materials we needed for the program. Five or six of my volunteer kitchen crew, and a couple of other helpers, piled into Audrie's van and my car and off we went to Grand Island, where the Student Union building had been made available to us. It worked well because there were no classes at the college that week.

We began the day, as we usually did at such times, with a weekday morning service. Sunday is a weekday in the Jewish scheme of things. The greater Nebraska folks liked that part of these events a lot. They rarely had a chance to be part of the group doing Jewish worship. After the service we took a little break for what people in my family called, when I was growing up, "Coffee and…" That

New York Deli Comes to the Prairie

meant there were pastries or cookies to go along with the coffee. On this day we had pieces of Entenmann's, the closest we could get to the Danish pastries every diner in New York might serve. Then we moved on to the first learning session of the day, a film about life in the old Lower East Side, followed by a discussion. Then we held a second session that had to do with the waves of immigration that had created the Jewish American experience.

While we were engaged in our learning sessions the kitchen crew was busy unloading the food. There was thin-sliced corned beef, pastrami, and turkey. Mountains of it. Kosher dill pickles, coleslaw, potato salad, potato k'nishes, containers of spicy deli mustard, and squeeze bottles of the Russian dressing that some delis served on their corned beef sandwiches. We had bought cases of diet and regular soda. A coffee urn was brewing and there was another with hot water for tea. The kitchen crew put out all the disposable plates, cutlery, and cups. The college had loaned us a portable steam table for the hot items. Everything was ready to go by the time the morning's learning sessions were completed.

There was great anticipation felt by everyone as we made our way to the area in which the eating of all these delectables would happen. The enticing aromas of hot, thin-sliced deli meats wafted through the air from the steam table. When we got there and people started to form lines to get their lunches, somebody shouted out that we should say the blessing before eating. It was a Jewish event, after all. So I taught the group a blessing different than the usual one. In translation it is: "Blessed is our eternal sovereign God of the universe by whose thought all things come into being." When that was finished, the group let out a roaring Amen and then proceeded to make up their plates. Barney Greengrass had sent so much food that anybody who wished to was able to make up a package to take home with them at the end of the day.

We ended our program that day with one of the members of my synagogue who played guitar leading the group in singing, mostly songs everyone knew. We had what we called a friendship circle

Mr. Levine and Me

with everyone standing in a big circle and having an opportunity to say something about how they felt about our day. That was a lovely moment. And then the day was over.

We distributed the doggie bags people had made up and labeled with their names earlier, did a cleanup of the area, bid everyone safe travels, loaded everything back into Audrey's van, piled into our vehicles, and made our way back to Lincoln. We were all very happy with how the day had gone. Audrey, who had done most of the planning, got loads of compliments. I remember feeling very good about the day, and very tired on the way back.

Several years later I was visiting my son, Dan, who lived in New York. We were walking around on a chilly November day. He suggested we stop somewhere for something to eat or a bowl of soup. We were on the East Side, so I suggested Barney Greengrass, which I'd always thought had the best barley mushroom soup. I didn't recall, just then, that deli's role in the success of a greater Nebraska event. We took a cab uptown to 86th Street and went into the deli. There were half a dozen deli men behind the counter, busily slicing corned beef or pastrami and assembling sandwiches. Across from the counter there were perhaps fifteen or twenty tables. Dan and I sat down, ordered our soup, and enjoyed every drop.

When we got ready to leave I took our check to the front, where an elderly man was seated behind the cash register. I handed him the check and noticed, tacked to the bulletin board behind him, a copy of an article from a Grand Island newspaper that had been written about our event years before. The headline was: "New York Deli Comes to the Prairie."

I was amazed. Everything you read above came flowing into my consciousness, and I remembered in that moment sending the article to Barney Greengrass shortly after the event. To the side of the article was a picture of me, Audrey, and my volunteer kitchen crew standing next to a table filled with deli food. Even in the grainy newspaper photo it looked good enough to eat.

New York Deli Comes to the Prairie

As I gave the cashier (who was, I think, Barney Greengrass himself) the money to pay for our soup, I pointed out the article hanging on the bulletin board behind him. I said, "That's me, and the food on the table came from here." He looked at it, read my name beneath the picture, and then shouted out to his customers and workers, "Hey everybody! We got a rabbi from Nebraska!" For some reason, the people in the deli gave a round of applause.

My son knew I was no celebrity. He smiled, none the less.

The Seed Corn of Life

After I'd completed my first semester of studies at the seminary, Hebrew Union College in New York, I was heading home on the commuter bus that I rode from New York to New Jersey each day during my first year of school. I'd gotten in the habit of getting my reading done on the bus and on this day I was reading something by Erik Erikson, "Childhood and Society." I was sitting next to a sort of chubby man with gray curly hair, a round red face, and a pleasant way about him. We said hello and exchanged a couple of words before I started my reading. After a few minutes he asked me what I was reading and I showed him the cover of the book. Then he asked me why I was reading that book, so I told him it was for a class. He asked where I was going to school. I really wanted him to stop asking me questions, but he was a nice enough person and I certainly didn't want to offend him. So I told him I was studying in the Cantorial program at the Hebrew Union College. He lit up when he heard that. The next thing he said to me a few minutes later was that he was the chairman of the youth education committee at his synagogue and wondered if we could exchange phone numbers so he could call if they ever needed a substitute teacher for one of the children's classes. I told him my name and gave him my number. He told me his name, Harris, and I went back to my reading.

The following week I got a call from him. He told me his eighth-grade teacher would not be there on the coming Sunday and asked if I could fill in. I asked him what the class was studying, and he said he'd have a lesson plan ready for me and some materials for the kids. I went into the synagogue that Sunday, spent an hour with

The Seed Corn of Life

a half dozen eighth graders, got paid thirty dollars for my trouble, and went home. It was a pleasant time. I enjoyed being with those eighth graders.

During the next week Harris called me and told me the teacher I had substituted for had decided to leave. He asked if I would take the class for the rest of the school year, another couple of months. I agreed, and just like that I was the new eighth-grade teacher. The class sessions usually revolved around a particular topic, but sometimes the discussions happened in unplanned ways. These were bright children, full of questions, doubts, and the unsureness as well as the sureness of youth. It was intellectually stimulating for me to be working with them. Sometimes I wondered just who was teaching who.

Near the end of one of our class sessions, during which we had been discussing the meaning of some of the mourning customs in the Jewish tradition, one of the kids asked a pretty profound question. "We sort of know what death is," she said, "but we don't know what life is. Do you think we could talk about both life and death sometime? What is life, anyway?" Wow, that was heavy! I told her and the class I'd think about that and figure out some way to bring that discussion to the class before the school year ended. And then that class ended. "See you next week," I said, and we all headed home.

I thought about that eighth-grade girl's question quite a few times over the next few weeks. It was a difficult question to answer. The rabbi of my childhood, Rabbi Klein, came to mind. I remembered him giving me the best answer at the time. He just said he didn't know. Maybe, I thought, that might be best. But I was interested in having that discussion, and a lesson plan was beginning to take shape in my mind. A few days later I went to a garden store and bought some seed corn, hard little kernels, discolored and cracked. I also went to a convenience store and bought some Bull Durham tobacco, the kind that comes in a little cloth bag with a drawstring.

Mr. Levine and Me

Some people used that to hand roll cigarettes. I dumped out the tobacco and filled the little bag with the dried-up corn kernels.

When I got to class on the Sunday following my purchases I began in the usual way, checking off the names of the kids who were there in my attendance book. I was glad everyone was present. Either their parents were doing a good job, or the kids liked their teacher (I preferred to think it was the second option). Then one of the boys led the class in a song that he accompanied on his guitar. It was one of the many versions of "Oseh Shalom, the Maker of Peace." Everyone, even those who didn't know this version, joined in once he had played it through a couple of times.

After that we moved on to the lesson. I said that today we were going to try and figure out what it means when we say "dead" or "alive." First we talked about what things we think of as being dead. One of the boys said boulders were dead. I asked him why and he said that boulders don't move, they just sit there forever. I wrote the word 'boulder' on the chalkboard. Somebody else said that wood was dead and gave the same reasons. One of the others said sometimes people were dead and related a story about how she had gone to a funeral at a church to be with friends of her family at a sad time. The funeral was for the grandfather of one of her friends. Unlike at a Jewish funeral, the coffin was open, and everyone walked by it to pay last respects to the one who was laid out in it. She said it was obvious that it was a dead person. I wrote the words 'wood' and 'person' on the board under 'boulder.'

"So, what's alive?" I asked.

The kids laughed. Everyone knows what's alive. *People, pets, plants, trees, birds, animals, bugs, spiders, snakes*. I wrote all those words and a few more on the board in a new column. Then I asked how they knew these things were alive. There was a torrent of answers.

"Of course they're alive. They move, they breathe, they grow, they reproduce." There was a little snickering here. Then one of the boys said something profound. "They die."

The Seed Corn of Life

The room fell silent for a minute. It was as if those vibrant eighth-grade boys and girls were contemplating their own mortality for the first time. I think it was a major moment of awakening for some, or maybe all of them. After another couple of minutes talking about what had gone on before in the discussion, it was time to bring out my props and see what would happen.

I took out the Bull Durham bag filled with seed corn and placed it on the table. "I want to show you something and let you think about it for a minute." I dumped the kernels onto the table around which we were seated and asked, "Tell me, are these alive or dead?" The students peered at the kernels for a time. One of them asked if they could touch them. I have a feeling some of the kids may have thought I was playing some kind of joke on them. The kernels didn't move. They didn't breathe. They just stayed where they had been put down on the table. After a time one of the kids said, "It's obvious they're dead." And I said, "Are you sure?" He looked a little confused when I said that. After a pretty long silence I said, "They're alive. They're not moving. They're not breathing. They're just staying where we put them. But they're alive, for sure."

I got up and went to the supply cabinet and took out eight flowerpots and a bag of potting soil I had stashed there before the kids arrived. I got the students to fill the pots with soil and told them they should place three or four of the kernels in each about an inch and a half deep and add a little water to each pot. When they were finished I told them they had planted seed corn that looked like old, cracked pebbles, dead things to be sure. Then I said that boulders and wood have an atomic structure of electrons and neutrons and other particles that science tells us are constantly moving. Just because we can't see that movement with our eyes doesn't mean it isn't happening. "So," I asked, "If it's moving is it really dead?" I went on to say that anything that dies—animal, bird, insect, plant, or person—eventually decomposes and turns to earth and somehow becomes, again, a part of the never-ending story of life.

Mr. Levine and Me

When I finished with all of that, I told the class that if we put the flowerpots on the windowsill and made sure they got water now and then, little corn plants would begin to emerge before the end of the school year. I'm not sure if the kids really believed me even then. They had planted little malformed and cracked pebbles. Each week thereafter, though, some of those great children would go to the windowsill to check on the flowerpots when they arrived each Sunday morning until one day one of them shouted, "Hey, come here, look at this." All the students went to the windowsill to see the amazing little green sprouts, which had awakened from their sleep. They were excited. It was not said, but I knew they were getting a look at the miracle of life.

We never really answered the questions about what life is or what death is, but we gained something to think about. And I was so grateful that Harris had asked me what I was reading that afternoon on the commuter bus.

Off to Oaxaca

When I returned to the United States after my three wonderful years in New Zealand, I had visions of establishing a retreat center somewhere. I had been a practitioner of mindfulness meditation for a long time, and I thought that perhaps I could share a little of what I had been taught by some wise people over the years. I had limited funds so I knew it would not be easy to do what I was thinking of doing. I began trying to find a suitable place online and I actually found a few that would have worked, even some in upstate New York with a price tag I could afford. But after further investigation it became clear to me that the places with reasonable prices needed major work of one kind or another. I knew I'd be unable to do that with my limited resources.

One day, during my online search, I came across a mini hotel for sale in the little village of San Agustinillo in Oaxaca, Mexico. I pored over the photographs of the place. It had five sleeping rooms with kitchenettes, each of which could accommodate four or five people, as well as a two-bedroom apartment, where the owners lived. The ground level was an open space that was being used as an Internet cafe. I saw that as perfect for a meditation space. There were vending machines along one wall and an ice cream freezer. And, according to the listing online, the place had one of the few telephones in the village. The exterior of the building was white stucco. The front entrance faced the main road that ran through the village, and the rear of the building looked out on the Pacific Ocean and provided access to the beach.

As I looked at the photos and read the descriptions I began to get excited. Maybe, I thought, I had found the perfect place. The next day I contacted the person listed as the owner, Julia, and we talked about the hotel for maybe an hour. My Spanish was not the greatest and I was happy that Julia was fluent in English. While we were talking I asked why she wanted to sell the hotel. She told me that she and her husband, Alphonso, did not really want to sell it; the hotel had been their dream. But, she said, her husband's father, who lived in Guadalajara, an eighteen-hour drive from San Agustinillo, had become ill and needed them to return there to look after him. She and Alphonso were heartbroken at the prospect of giving up their dream, but they both knew it was their duty to take care of Alphonso's father. I was touched by the strength of their love for him.

By the time we reached the end of our conversation we had agreed that it would be good if I came for a visit before I made a decision, so I booked a room in the mini hotel beginning in two weeks. I booked it for six weeks because I wanted to have enough time to be sure I'd enjoy living there before making the major commitment to move and establish myself and my retreat center in the southwestern part of Mexico. Over the next few days, as I got ready for my journey, I thought about all the ways I would try to market my retreat center at the beach. I had fantasies of offering retreats to burned out Wall Streeters and other professionals who needed a time of peaceful reflection.

When the time came to travel I flew from Lincoln to Chicago to Mexico City, and then to a place called Huatulco, where I rented a car and drove the fifty or so miles to San Agustinillo. As I got to the village I saw that it was even nicer than the listing had shown me. There were nice homes along the main road and on the ridge above. The ocean was serene and beautiful in its blue splendor. I parked and went into the Internet cafe, where I was greeted by an attractive Mexican woman who introduced herself as Julia, the person I had spoken with on the phone about the hotel. I told her who I was and she hugged me warmly. "Bienvenido, Miguel," she almost shouted. She said something in a language I didn't understand at all to a young Indio woman who I guessed was an employee. That woman looked at me and said, "Llave?" I knew enough Spanish to realize

The Seed Corn of Life

she was asking me for my key. I gave it to her and she went out to the car and came back with my carryon bag, the only luggage I had brought along for my six-week stay. Julia said "Cuarto tres" to her employee, and the young woman disappeared carrying my bag up the stairs on the outside of the building to Room 3.

I went to bed early that evening because I was really tired after my long journey from Chicago. I kept the windows in Room 3 open, and the sound of the waves lapping against the shore provided the perfect sound for good sleeping. When I awoke in the morning I was totally refreshed and well rested. I brewed some coffee with a small stovetop espresso pot, had a quick shower as it brewed, got dressed, drank the coffee, and headed out. When I opened the door there was a cute little black and white dog laying across the threshold of my room. I wondered whose dog it might be. When I went down the stairs the dog followed close behind. He went with me everywhere I went that day.

I had breakfast at a little cafe with a sign out front that read: "CAFE - Lavandaria." It was an odd combination. Cafe and Laundry. But that is what it was. You could drop your laundry off there and have a coffee or something to eat, and people who worked there would take care of your laundry and drop it off dried and folded at your home or at the hotel if you liked. The dog stayed with me, laying at my feet. I gave it some of my scrambled eggs and a bit of toast. He ate it and lay back down. I liked that little dog.

I learned later that day from Julia that the dog was named Loco and belonged to Eduardo, the current mayor of San Agustinillo. Loco had apparently adopted me. He was my little companion for almost all the time I was there. I had many good experiences and sweet interactions with people there during my six-week stay, with Loco almost always at my side.

I'd like to tell you about some of them. I think of them as friends even though I know I'll never see them again.

Fishing with Eduardo

Eduardo was the mayor, not because he had been elected, but because every few years the people of the village would have a meeting and try to convince someone to take the job. No one really wanted to be the mayor because no one wanted to deal with the red tape or with the Federales.

Eduardo was, like many of the men in San Agustinillo, a fisherman. Each Monday he and his helpers would go out in his oversized motorboat, which was built in such a way that it could be filled with water without sinking and become a sort of floating aquarium where the live catch could be kept alive until it could be sold. He and his helpers would drop long lines with many baited hooks along their length into the ocean. The lines would be attached to a buoy and left until the following Thursday, when Eduardo and his helpers would climb into the boat and go back out to haul in the lines, drop whatever had been caught into the water-filled boat, rebait the lines and toss them back into the sea, and then bring the live catch to the wholesale market in Puerto Angel, another village up the coast.

Early one morning as I was walking back to San Agustinillo from the next village down the road, Eduardo approached me and asked, "¿*Quieres trabajar hoy?*" He was asking me if I wanted to work, and of course I said yes. What a great opportunity for an old guy like me to experience a bit of the culture firsthand, I thought. So off I went with Eduardo and two of his helpers. The third helper had gotten sick and I was taking his place that day.

We spent the day hauling in the lines, heavy with fish. At one point we were surrounded by a school of dolphins. "*¡Delfines,*

Fishing with Eduardo

delfines!" One of the men shouted and we watched the dolphins leaping in and out of the water, doing the acrobatic ballet that dolphins do. I was amazed to be in such an amazing place.

At the end of the day Eduardo dropped me and one of the helpers off in San Agustinillo and went off with the other helper to Puerto Angel to sell the catch to a wholesaler. When he returned he tried to pay me my share of the money he had gotten for the day's catch, but I refused to take his money. I explained that I was just a visitor, a tourist having a good time, and thanked him for the great experience I'd had on his boat. I guessed Eduardo must have told everyone that I had refused his money. From that day until I left a couple weeks later no one in the village—the people who ran the restaurants, the cafe, the laundry, the bodega, any of them—allowed me to pay for anything. I'd never had such an experience before.

Eduardo had not only let Loco adopt me, but I think he got his friends all around the village to adopt me, too.

Loco and My Meditation Partners

One day when I was in the Internet cafe writing and sending out emails, someone came in with two little boys in tow. They looked me over pretty carefully since I was different from most of the tourists who passed through. Most tourists who came to San Agustinillo were Mexican people from nearby, like Huatulco, or from far away like Mexico City. There were rarely North Americans visiting there. I asked Julia if I could buy some ice cream for them and she asked their mother if it would be all right. The mother smiled and nodded, and Julia gave the boys ice cream on a stick. They were really happy about that. Loco was at my feet and when the boys finished with their ice cream they played with him while their mother made a phone call and I continued with my emailing. Julia set up a timer so that she'd know how much to charge for the call.

    The next day I was sitting on the beach under a thatched palapa doing my daily meditation. I was completely unaware of anything around me as I focused on my breath. *I breathe in, I breathe out, thoughts arise, I don't follow them, I breathe in, I breathe out...* At some point in my meditation I felt something on my leg that brought me out of my meditative state. I opened my eyes and there was Loco, licking my leg. I don't know how Loco could have known, but I noticed that my leg had been out from under the shade of the palapa and was getting pretty red. I wanted to believe that Loco was trying to save me from getting sunburned, but I knew that couldn't

Loco and My Meditation Partners

be. I looked around, and there behind me—sitting cross-legged—in the sand with their hands resting on their knees and thumbs touching forefingers, were the little boys I'd gotten ice cream for the previous day. They looked like perfect little meditators. "*¿Qué haces?*" ("What are you doing?") one of them asked. "*Mis meditaciones*," I replied. The little boys didn't know what I was talking about so they said something to one of the beach vendors who walked around with cold drinks for sale. She asked me what I was doing and I told her. Then she turned to the boys and said, "*Son sus devociones.*"

The boys understood that and put their hands together as if they were praying. Loco was laying with his paws out in front of him.

Was he praying too? I like to think he was.

My Big Family Goes to Museo de Tortuga

One day Julia told me there was a special place nearby that she thought I might like to see. It was Museo de Tortuga - Museum of the Tortoise. That afternoon I told her I was going to go and see it. The young Indio woman who had carried my bag up to Room 3 when I first arrived said something to Julia, who told me that the young woman had lived there her whole life and had never been to the museum. I told Julia I would be glad to take her. Julia said it cost ten pesos to get in, but children can go in free with their parents, and she knew the children would want to come, too. I told Julia to tell her employee, whose name I never learned, that she should go and get the children. I'd wait for her. Half an hour later she was back with her two children, and her sister and her three children. I smiled and opened the door of my pretty small rental car and all seven of them squeezed in somehow. They were all so excited.

The realization that these nice people couldn't afford the equivalent of one dollar to visit a museum in their community was a hard one for me. I could tell these young women were as happy as any people I'd ever known. They worked hard, earned very little money, but still managed to take care of whatever needed to be taken care of. They were lovely and their children were beautiful. I was so very glad they spent an afternoon with me.

As we drove to the museum, memories of my own childhood came to the fore. We were poor. There was never any extra money

My Big Family Goes to Museo de Tortuga

around. I wore my older brother's clothes when he outgrew them. We ate well because of my mother's cooking skills. She could make even the simplest ingredients into something good. My brother and I had to earn a little money from a young age if we expected to go to a movie or visit a bowling alley. We, like these two young women and their children, were poor, but we were also happy most of the time. I felt a kinship across the ages with them.

We wandered Museo de Tortuga together. The floors were made of beautiful multicolored tiles. The walls were a tan stucco adorned with lots of photographs of tortoises at various stages of their lives. There were also paintings of these wonderful sea animals here and there. In the middle of the main hall there was a large bronze sea tortoise with a rope barrier strung through silvery metal poles surrounding it. It was a beautiful place, filled with images of the natural world. I was glad Julia had told me about it.

I wondered, as I wandered through Museo de Tortuga with my entourage of young women and children, if people thought the women were my daughters and their children my grandchildren. It felt to me as if they could have been. We stopped to listen to a presentation, given along with a slide show, by a young man in the main hall of the museum. I understood not a word. The presenter was speaking *más rápido*. After that we went to the rear of the museum and pushed through the hanging plastic sheets to a series of breeding tanks in which baby tortoises were raised until they were big enough and strong enough to be released into the ocean. Each of the tanks had a good number of tortoises in them, and in each succeeding tank the tortoises were larger than in the previous one.

As we walked through the museum that day I always had a child holding each of my hands. I think they, like Loco and the two little meditator boys, had adopted me. When I realized a few days later that I would not be able to stay there in Oaxaca, I knew I would miss them all so very much. I think I was feeling love for all of them. Somehow they were family.

Leaving Paradise

I had been in San Agustinillo about four weeks. I'd spent a day working for the mayor. Two little boys must have thought I was okay, okay enough to imitate. Loco had adopted me. A couple of young Indio women and their children felt to me like daughters and grandchildren. I'd been invited to the village school's graduation ceremonies, which reminded me a lot of the one I'd attended at a Māori school in New Zealand. Julia treated me like family. I had great respect for her husband Alphonso and his devotion to his ailing father. It felt so good to be there.

I was just about to find myself an *abogado* (lawyer) to help me work out the details around the purchase of the mini hotel when I made a discovery that would cause me to change my mind.

As I mentioned in a previous story, I have had a pacemaker since 1990. I'm 100 percent dependent on it. I don't know why I waited until I had been in San Agustinillo more than four weeks before I investigated what medical services were available. It turned out that the nearest pacemaker clinic was several hours away from the village. That was, to me, too big a risk to take. I was disappointed for myself and even more disappointed for Julia and Alphonso. I felt like I was letting them down. It was difficult for me to explain to Julia that as much as I liked the place and loved the people, I just couldn't take a chance given my situation. I apologized to her that I had not checked this out earlier, even before I made my visit. She was so very gracious, saying it was no problem, that God would take care of them.

Leaving Paradise

When it came time for me to leave Julia walked me out to the car and gave me a hug and a kiss on each cheek. She smiled and told me it had been very good to meet me. I cried a little on the way to Huatulco. I flew to Mexico City, then Chicago, then Lincoln.

Two weeks later I got a letter from Julia. She wrote that God sent me to be her angel. After I left, she wrote, Alphonso's father suddenly got better and she believed that had something to do with me. She also wrote that because I was there to buy the hotel it had been taken off the market. No one was looking at it while I was there. And now they would be able to keep it. Alphonso was already making plans to bring his now healthy father to live with them. All was good in the world.

I reread Julia's letter several times and marveled at the many coincidences that had allowed her and her husband to keep their dream. I remembered an old saying someone had told me long ago: "Coincidences are the small miracles for which God takes no credit." I was happy that someone in Mexico thought I was an angel because of the coincidences that brought us together.

George Washington Carver James

When I was in high school a new guy turned up. His name was George Washington Carver James. George was a big muscular Black guy whose family had moved to New Haven from somewhere in upstate New York. He had been a Golden Gloves boxer when he lived in New York, but in spite of that, he was one of the most peaceful people I've known. Somehow George and I became friends and we would hang out together at school, at lunchtime in the drugstore on Whalley Avenue where there was a lunch counter, and sometimes in his neighborhood around Dixwell Avenue, a place where lots of white parents told their children not to go. It was a Black neighborhood, and even though people didn't think of themselves as racist or prejudiced, at the same time they discouraged their kids from being friends with people who were different. "Stay with your own kind" was a sort of watchword where I lived. My parents, like the parents of most everyone I knew, fell into this category.

When I was growing up, New Haven was a city of ethnic neighborhoods. I lived in one of them, in the midst of mostly Jews and Italians. There was a Puerto Rican area too. It was another place, like the black area around Dixwell Avenue, that white kids were warned away from. "Don't go there," parents would warn. "They've all got switchblade knives."

Even though George knew I was Jewish he told me it would be fun for me to visit the church his family attended on Dixwell

Avenue, the House of Prayer for All People, Inc., whose pastor was known as Daddy Grace. He said it would be different than anything I'd ever seen.

Even before George told me it would be fun to go there, I knew about the place. It had been in the news a few times when the House of Prayer for All People, Inc. bought an old building in East Haven that was built like a medieval castle perched near the top of a hill. It had once been the Castle Restaurant. It had its own beachfront and Daddy Grace was going to use it as a place for services and mass baptisms. The neighbors around there were not happy with the prospect of lots of Black people coming around, and some of them went to court to try and prevent it. All of that was reported in the daily paper. From an early time in my life I read the newspaper every day. I still read the *Times* every day online, and I miss turning the pages of the actual paper.

I was fascinated with this Dixwell Avenue church partly because of the news stories, partly because the place didn't really look like a church but rather a commercial building of some kind, but most of all because the preacher's name was Daddy Grace and the name of the church was the House of Prayer for All People, Inc.

On the Sunday morning that I went there the place was crowded with people. I think I was probably the only person in the place who wasn't Black. That didn't matter to me, and I could tell it didn't matter to anyone else, either. I sat in the rear of the church and after a while George saw me and came over to sit with me and wait for the service to begin.

We were talking about school and girls and other stuff when suddenly there was a drum roll and the doors at the rear of the sanctuary swung open. The band up front began to play a melody I'd heard before. I recognized it as "Sweet Georgia Brown," the theme song of the Harlem Globetrotters. Then a blue-robed choir entered clapping hands and singing "di dah dah dah dah dah dah dah dah, Sweet Daddy Grace." They did this over and over again as they sashayed their way down the center aisle and the outside aisles. When they

Mr. Levine and Me

got to the front and took their places on the stage, Daddy Grace himself entered. He was wearing a long gold robe and had a few necklaces on. For some reason, he seemed to me like a bride on her way to the altar on her wedding day as he walked—no, slow-danced—his way down the aisle as the music continued. When he reached the front and got behind the pulpit, the music and clapping abruptly stopped. Daddy Grace spoke loudly into the microphone, "Good morning church!" Everybody there responded with a roaring "Good Morning Sweet Daddy," and the service began. I stayed for maybe an hour or so before I told George I had to get going. I remember thinking that I never had that much fun at synagogue.

George was a year ahead of me in school and he graduated the following year. I decided at the end of my junior year that I was going to quit school. My parents were opposed, of course, but I finally wore them down. When they asked me what I planned to do with my life I told them I wanted to join the Army. They weren't happy about that either, but I think they believed it was a better path for me than just hanging around, so they signed whatever release was necessary for me to enlist at seventeen. When I told George about my plans he said that he was going to join the Army as well. He said his family thought it was a good idea since they couldn't afford to send him to college. That was a rationale many families had back then, and maybe still today as well.

George and I went to the Army recruiting station in a storefront downtown and enlisted together in a program called the "buddy plan." The idea was that the Army would guarantee we would serve together throughout our enlistment. So George and I went first to Fort Dix, New Jersey, for basic training and then to Fort Sill, Oklahoma, for specialty training.

At Fort Sill, George and I sometimes managed to get out of some duty we didn't want to do because George had figured out that if we walked around the base looking like we knew what we were doing nobody would question us. He bought a clipboard from the PX and carried it with him when we were skipping something. He thought the clipboard would make us look official. On the couple occasions when we were stopped and questioned by some lieutenant it was always "What are you men doing?" And George would glance at the clipboard and respond, "Checking details, sir." And the answer from the Lieutenant was always, "All right. Carry on."

It was during that period that I had to take bereavement leave to attend the funeral of my stepfather, Morris. At first I didn't realize it was Morris who had died. I got called to the orderly room where a corporal handed me a telegram from the Red Cross. It read something like, "Father dead in New Haven. Make travel and bereavement leave arrangements." I was surprised to get this message since I hadn't had much to do with my father since he left my mother when I was about three years old. Over the years, from that time until when I got that telegram, I hadn't been around my father more than a half dozen or so times. When I called my mother she told me it wasn't my father who had died but Morris, my stepfather. I was really saddened to hear that. My mother had married Morris when I was about six years old and he had been the person I thought of as my father ever since.

When I got to my mother's home in New Haven she told me that Morris had committed suicide by going to New York and leaping from the Manhattan Bridge.

Childhood memories filled me up. I remembered that when my father left my mother she placed my sister and brother and me in an orphanage until she could get herself on her feet. My sister stayed there for about a year until my mother was able to take her home. She was seven years older than me and was better able to take care of herself than either my brother or me. He and I remained in the orphanage another couple of years until after Morris and my mother were married. When we were sprung from the orphanage we went to live in Guilford, about twenty miles from New Haven, on a chicken farm that was owned by my grandfather's best friend, Nicola, from the old country (Uncle Nick's chicken farm, as has come up previously in these pages). Life went from bad to good the moment I knew I'd be getting out of the orphanage.

When I returned to Fort Sill after Morris' funeral I learned that my unit had shipped out to Germany and the buddy system was over. I ended up at Fort Bragg, North Carolina.

I lost touch with George Washington Carver James and never saw him again. Years later I learned from someone who had known us both that he had become a lawyer, gotten married, and moved with his family to somewhere down south. But I've always remembered what he used to say when we were goofing off. "Checking details, sir."

I've spent the rest of my life checking details, not to get out of duty, but to better know what I was doing and maybe who I was becoming.

I'm from Nebraska

One day while I was working on my sermon for the next Sabbath service I got a call from a friend. She told me there had been some vandalism at a nearby mosque and she asked me if I would go there at noontime to demonstrate support from the Jewish community. I said I would be there, and at noon I was in front of the mosque with thirty or forty others—Muslims from other mosques, Christians, and Jews who had turned out to support this community. The mosque was small, housed in a storefront. I knew a couple of the Muslim people in the crowd and commiserated with them. I think we spoke about similar things that had happened from time to time at some of the area synagogues. We all had much in common. It was a chilly day and someone from the mosque was busy bringing cups of coffee to the people standing out in the cold. That community had been in the neighborhood for quite a long time and had never been attacked like this before. Both of the front windows had been smashed. There was some very nasty graffiti painted on the door and on the sidewalk. The least offensive of that graffiti read: "GO BACK WHERE YOU CAME FROM." The people of the mosque were dismayed and terrified.

When I noticed the shards of glass scattered all over the sidewalk I remembered things I had read of long ago about the night of terror in prewar Germany that came to be known as Kristallnacht, the "Night of Broken Glass." On that tragic night and during the days that followed just about every Jewish synagogue and business in Germany had been attacked in a preview of the very bad times to come with the Nazis in control of the country. That happened on the ninth of November, 1938. I remembered reading that more than a thousand synagogues were burned or heavily damaged that night. Jewish-owned businesses all over the country were ransacked, and about a hundred Jewish people were killed. The police and fire companies were instructed to stand by and watch as building after building was burned to the ground, and the police were ordered to arrest the victims rather than the perpetrators. Thirty thousand people suffered that fate and were sent to concentration camps that would later become the death camps where they would be murdered by the Nazi regime. It came to me as I was thinking about this that, in the European way of numbering dates, November 9 is rendered as 9/11. I hoped we weren't now seeing the beginnings of such horrors on the streets of New York City.

The vandalism at this small mosque in the heart of Queens was, in my opinion, the result of the heated anti-Muslim rhetoric that had become so common in our country. It was, for me, a frightening prospect. Americans of every stripe found ways to blame all Muslims for the tragedy of our 9/11. The Muslim community of today, Americans all, like the German Jewish community of the 1930s and 40s, Germans all, had been blamed for all the ills in their countries in different eras.

As I was musing about all this, standing outside the desecrated mosque in Queens, a small man, wearing a typical Muslim hat that looked much like the Russian kippah I sometimes liked to wear, arrived. He introduced himself as Shamsi Ali and spoke a few words to the gathering. He said he was grateful that people from the non-Muslim community were there to show their support. He was articulate and calm. When he was finished I introduced myself to him and he told me he was the Imam of a mosque in another part of Queens. When I learned he was originally from Indonesia I felt a connection with him. I told him how warmly I had been welcomed there during my two visits to that country. We exchanged business cards and embraced Arab-style, with kisses on the cheeks. Shamsi left at that point. He had to visit other mosques in the area to try and reassure their members with the hope that this vandalism would be an isolated incident.

After a while, when the police officers who were posted there gave the okay, we all helped clean up the debris on the sidewalk in front of the mosque. Someone handed me a push broom and I began to sweep the bits of broken glass into little piles. Thoughts of Kristallnacht crept back into my mind. Other people scooped up the shimmering shards of glass with dustpans or pieces of cardboard. Soon the sidewalk in front of the mosque was clean. The windows were still gaping holes, but someone was already painting over the graffiti on the door.

I went back to my office and finished up the sermon I had been working on. And life went on. I suppose that's the way it is. Something happens, you respond to it, and then you get back to what you were doing. This time was different though. Those Holocaust images that the attack on the mosque brought to the forefront of my thoughts kept buzzing around my mind.

A couple of weeks later Shamsi called me. He told me that two of the members of his mosque had been beaten up by some men who were shouting anti-Muslim slurs. Thankfully, he told me, neither of those men had been too seriously injured, but his community was in a state of shock and fear. He asked if I would come the next day and speak with his community during morning prayers. If I did so, he thought, the people of his community would know that they were not hated by everyone. I agreed to do it.

The following day I drove to Shamsi's mosque in another part of Queens and found a parking space on a side street a block away. I made my way to the mosque, entered and removed my shoes, and found a place near the rear of the prayer room to sit on the floor with the others who were there. I was wearing my Russian kippah and I guess I fit in. As the prayer service went on I just did what everyone else was doing. I stood when they did, bowed when they did, dropped down to my knees and touched my forehead to the floor as they did. I didn't know a word of Arabic but I have to say the way of Muslim prayer is very meditative, very focused, and somehow calming.

When it came to the part of the service where remarks were to be given, Shamsi Ali stood and from behind the lectern said, "My friend Rabbi Michael is supposed to be here but he must be late. I don't see him." I stood up from my place in the rear of the prayer room and said, "I'm here, Shamsi." I began walking to the front, stepping between the people who were still sitting on the prayer mats. The man I'd been sitting next to smiled and said, "You are the Rabbi? I thought you were Muslim." I smiled back at him and made my way to the front.

I spoke for about ten minutes about our need to respect one another and not let the behavior of a few bad people turn us away from doing the right thing. I told them they would be welcome to visit my synagogue if they wished, and that they would be as welcome there as I felt myself to be among them. I ended my remarks with "Salaam Aleikum," which is the Arabic rendering of the Hebrew "Shalom Aleichem." The words mean "peace be upon you." Shamsi thanked me for coming and told me that it meant a lot to him and to his community.

I left the mosque after lots of expressions of thanks and brotherhood and began to make my way back to my car. As I approached the side street where I'd parked, a pickup truck pulled out. Whoever was on the passenger side rolled down his window and shouted the same words I'd seen a few weeks before painted on the door of the vandalized mosque: "Go back where you came from!" My Russian kippah had fooled him, I guess. I shouted back at him, "I'm from Nebraska!" The truck sped off with a screeching of tires.

Later that same year I asked Shamsi if he would deliver the address during the observance of Yom Hashoah, the solemn time of remembrance for the victims of the Holocaust, and he accepted my invitation. When I informed the members of my board they were not happy about it. "How can you ask a Muslim to do that?" was a question I heard a number of times. They didn't prevent me from going ahead with my plans, though, and on the appointed day Shamsi, in his quiet, peaceful way, delivered what I thought was the perfect speech. One of the things he said was that it was only the Jews who could understand the hatred that was swirling around the Muslim community because the Jews had experienced it and so much more. When he finished his address the congregation stood and gave him an extended ovation.

When everything was drawing to a close I stood beside my friend Shamsi. I thanked him for the wonderful talk he had given and ended my remarks by saying that he could easily be my rabbi. Shamsi smiled, and then said, "Maybe your rabbi thinks I could be his rabbi, but I know that he is my imam."

Ritchie Lyman and the Quest for Equality

It was 1955, and I was in junior high school. We had classes that were required like English, Math, History, and Science, and we also had elective classes we could choose. The way my school took care of how students chose their elective classes was pretty smart in those days, before there were computers. A week or two before the school year was set to begin, signup sheets were placed on bulletin boards in the hallways of the school. One hallway had the seventh-grade choices, another those for eighth grade, and another those for the ninth. Each signup sheet had numbered lines and students would come to the school building, wander up and down their grade's designated hallway, look over the class offerings, and make their choices. When all the lines of a signup sheet were filled in with students' names, the elective class on that page was closed. It was a simple and effective process. I think that low-tech system was somehow easier and worked better than the postcard mailings back and forth and the subsequent data-entry system at the beginning of the computer age. Call me a luddite if you want, but I think I'm right about this.

One of my junior high buddies, a kid named Richie Lyman, walked over to the school with me on elective class signup day. On the way there he came up with the crazy idea that we should sign up for Home Ec., a class that no boys were ever enrolled in. I laughed at the idea but Ritchie persisted. He said it would be fun to see how the office would react. Remember this was 1955, a time when only girls needed to learn how to cook, bake, and sew; how to use a vacuum cleaner or iron clothes; how to keep an orderly house. Boys went to wood shop or metal shop where they learned to use wood lathes, band saws, and other tools so that they could make things like cutting boards and birdhouses, or useless boxes made of sheet metal made with tin snips and soldering irons. So that day Ritchie and I wrote our names on one of the signup sheets and officially signed up for Home Ec., which was typed on the mimeographed signup sheet as "Home Economics."

A few days later the vice principal of our school (I still remember his name for some reason, Mr. Carr) called our parents and told them we needed to come to the school and take care of signing up for our elective classes. Our parents thought we had either forgotten or had blown off that little responsibility. Ritchie and I both knew what was going on. Mr. Carr was going to tell us we couldn't sign up for Home Ec. When we got to the school we waited outside Mr. Carr's office for a while and then the secretary told us we could go in. Mr. Carr was sitting behind his desk wearing his suit and his bow tie. He looked the same near the end of summer vacation as he did every day during the school year. He looked at us sitting across from him and smiled. "C'mon fellas," he said, "you know you can't take Home Ec. That's a girls' class." Ritchie was ready with an answer. "Mr. Carr," he said, "Home Ec. is open to eighth and ninth graders. That's what it says in the catalogue. There's nothing about girls only. That's the class we want to take."

Mr. Carr stopped smiling. We could tell he was getting aggravated. When he finally spoke again it was with a very quiet, ominous voice. "Okay boys, you're right. Just remember that when all your friends start laughing at you for being in a girlie class I won't be letting you transfer out. You will be stuck there for the whole year. Are you ready to change your minds about this?"

I looked at Ritchie. Ritchie looked at me. Then we both looked at Mr. Carr. It was as if Ritchie and I had read each other's minds. We said, almost in unison, "We want to stay in Home Ec." Mr. Carr glared at us for a few moments and then said, "Okay. Just remember what I told you. You're in Home Ec. for the year. Don't come whining to me. You've made your decision."

Ritchie and I laughed about our encounter with Mr. Carr as we walked back to our neighborhood. We laughed about his bow tie. We laughed about his threat. We laughed about how Ritchie had outsmarted him. And then we realized that we had to go to Home Ec. with the girls. We stopped laughing.

When classes began that fall and the time came for Ritchie and me to attend the first Home Ec. class any boy had ever attended in the history of our school, we entered the class with a bit of trepidation.

We went into the room warily. There were a couple of counters with kitchen sinks. There were several gas ranges and another counter with a few stand mixers and canisters with cooking tools in them. Vacuum cleaners were lined up against one of the walls. Part of the floor was covered in linoleum and part in carpet. There was a washing machine, something no one I knew had in their home, against one wall, and desks lined up in a second room that could be closed off with a movable folding wall. The room was filled with girls, all chattering away, and a female teacher seated at her desk. We knew it was time for class to begin when the teacher picked up a bell from her desk and shook it back and forth as if she were the schoolmarm in an old western movie. Ritchie and I found two seats next to each other. I think we were feeling a need for support in this alien environment. We were surrounded by girls. We'd never experienced that before. I couldn't have said these words then—I didn't even know the term at the time—but looking back I can only describe that first experience in Home Ec. as being trapped in some mysterious environment that could have been called "estrogen central."

The Home Ec. class met on Mondays, Wednesdays, and Fridays each week. At first Ritchie and I just listened and kept quiet. But after a week or so we became more comfortable with our surroundings. Mr. Carr had been right that some of our friends would razz us about being in a girlie class. Some of them called us names that wouldn't pass muster in a more politically correct era. We stuck it out anyway and it didn't take long before we were really a part of the class. Wearing an apron wasn't so bad. Cleaning the pans we baked cakes in was okay, too. Learning about how to manage a household, everything from shopping lists to balancing a checkbook to using a vacuum cleaner were all things that, for me at least, would become valuable skills as I moved through the years of my life.

The best thing about the experience was that, because Ritchie and I were in Home Ec. with twenty-five girls, we got to know them as people. They were friends instead of objects of desire. We ended up liking them for who they were and they liked us for who we were. There was no competition, no angst, no moves to try out, no lines to spout, no envy, no jealousy. It was just a bunch of kids learning together, having a good time baking cakes, or learning how to iron a shirt without burning it.

And oh yes, because we got to know so many girls we always had girls to see a movie with or go for ice cream, things that might have looked like dates to others, but which were really more like outings with friends.

Ritchie's father was an insurance agent and he took a new job in Hartford. Ritchie and his family moved there the summer after our Home Ec. experience. We didn't stay in touch, but I remember Ritchie Lyman. It was a good thing he had done when he talked me into signing up for Home Ec. I think that because he did that, at least partly because he did that, I've had more female friends than male friends throughout my life. Friends that were really friends and not objects.

It was a wonderful gift Ritchie gave me that summer day so long ago as we made our way to elective class signup day at our junior high. The following school year about twenty boys signed up. The year after I finished junior high and moved on to high school, Home Economics was listed, officially, as a co-ed class. Ritchie and I didn't think of it at the time, though I wish we had. We were pioneers, in our small way, in the ongoing quest for equality.

The Quintessential Jewish Festival

I first met the Monseigneur in the early 1990s, when he was the headmaster of Pius X High School. When I used his title he told me not to be so formal and said that Ivan would be fine. The first time I saw his school was when I was being given a tour of the city by one of the members of the synagogue search committee that was considering asking me to come and serve as the spiritual leader of the congregation. As we approached Pius X, the man laughed and said how wonderful it was that Lincoln was such a progressive city. "Look at that," he said as we got near the school. "We've even got a Black Muslim high school." It sounded like a well-worn joke, but we both got a chuckle out of it.

Sometime after coming to work in Lincoln I got a call from Ivan. He asked me if I could speak with one of the classes about the Jewish religion and point up some of the differences and similarities between it and the Catholicism the majority of the students at his school practiced. Of course I agreed. I've always thought that interfaith activities of all kinds were worthwhile. For the next few years I came to Pius X to give a similar lesson to one of the classes there. I enjoyed doing it and I thought the students enjoyed it too.

A couple years into my tenure with the synagogue I opened our community Passover Seder to people from the non-Jewish community. I had room for about one hundred at the Seder celebration, and usually about eighty or so of the synagogues' members attended the

The Quintessential Jewish Festival

event. I reasoned we could easily accommodate another twenty. I had already gotten a volunteer kitchen crew together a few years earlier for Seders, Chanukah dinners, and holiday and Sabbath celebrations, so the cooking part of the Seder was well taken care of. But when I put out the word that people from outside the congregation would be welcome to attend, the reservations came flying in. My usual eighty or so from the congregation had made their reservations but a hundred and twenty more from the non-Jewish community had also reserved a place at the Seder. The list had grown to about two hundred. As I said, we had room for about a hundred. I was going to have to either turn some of the people away or find a larger space.

Ivan had ended his work as headmaster and had become the person in charge of facilities at the church's cathedral. There was a school there as well. So I called him and explained my predicament. He was more than willing and happy to help out. We got together and discussed what would be needed. He told me not to worry about the setup of the space, which would be the cafeteria of the school. We drew out a plan for the space and he said he'd get some of the older kids to get the room properly set up. He also said it would be easier if I and my kitchen crew did the cooking in their commercial kitchen rather than cooking at the synagogue and having to bring everything over there. The person who ran the cafeteria would come and show us how everything worked in the kitchen and provide extra help if we needed it. I was so grateful for everything the Monseigneur was doing for us.

When the time came for the Seder, the second evening of Passover, I went to the Cathedral early to make sure we hadn't forgotten anything. I'd been cooking with my kitchen crew with help from a couple of the church's employees for most of the day and had gone home to change out of my kitchen clothes and into something more appropriate. When I went into the cafeteria it was set up perfectly: Three eight-foot tables were set up on a raised platform and another twenty tables were fanned out in front of that long head table in such a way that everyone would be able to see what was going on.

It took a while for the room to fill with people but little by little everyone found seats. At the head table were a couple of priests, members of the kitchen crew, a few of the young people who had helped with the set up, and a friend of mine who was a Lutheran pastor from a nearby community. Ivan was seated one chair away from my Lutheran buddy, and the chair between them was reserved for me.

I took my seat and looked out at the array of tables. Each of them was set beautifully. A vase of mixed flowers was in the center of each table. In front of each chair there was a copy of the community Haggadah, the book that is used to tell the story of the Exodus in the traditional way with story, song, readings, and poetry. I'd created this version a few years earlier. Everything looked perfect and very beautiful as well.

Ivan turned to me and asked if he could welcome everyone. I thought that was a great idea, since he represented the cathedral and he and the cathedral were our gracious hosts. Ivan stood and tapped his finger on the microphone as he tried to quiet everyone down. After a while, the conversations around the room stopped and the place was very quiet. Ivan welcomed everyone and thanked me for letting the cathedral host such a wonderful event. He told the gathered people that he had worked with me on several things in the past and had hopes our relationship would continue. It was a lovely talk. Then he said and did something I think I will never forget.

Ivan paused for a few moments and signaled to one of the young people who had helped with the set up. That person got up and headed to the back of the room. A half dozen others joined him. When they had all reached the rear of the room Ivan continued. "Tonight we are celebrating Passover. We are here together, Jews and Christians, to celebrate the eternal message of freedom. But we all must remember, especially those of us who are Christian, that this is the quintessential celebration of the Jewish faith. It is Jewish

The Quintessential Jewish Festival

through and through. So this evening we must all be Jews." Ivan took a yarmulka out of his pocket and placed it on his head and the young people who had gone to the rear of the room moved quickly between the rows of tables and handed each person a black silky yarmulka. What a wonderful gesture that was.

I had not known that Ivan was going to do that. I wondered for a moment where he had gotten all those yarmulkas. Then I thought, "I've been involved in interfaith work most of my life, but I think tonight I've been out-interfaithed."

It felt wonderful to come in second.

HUAC Comes to Town

In 1956, the House Un-American Activities Committee (HUAC) came to New Haven to conduct hearings. They set up shop at the federal courthouse downtown. The local papers reported this and most of the adults in my family were very worried about it.

I was living in the Legion Avenue neighborhood then. It was a so-called working-class neighborhood filled with Jews and Italians. In its own way it was a vibrant place. Stores lined two or three blocks of Legion Avenue. There was a grocery, Max Wax and Sons; a butcher shop, Barney Breyer; three bakeries just about next to each other on one block, Levine's, Tchaikovsky's, and Omer's, and another, Celentano's, just a block away. There was Mrs. Goldstein's produce market and Mr. Kaplan's fruit store. There was also M & T Appetizing, which sold all kinds of smoked fish and other delicacies; a luncheonette; a sundries store; and a little hardware store. Most of the stores on the avenue were Jewish owned and their customers were the Italian and Jewish people of the neighborhood. The Italians mostly identified as Siciliano, and most of the Jews hailed from places in Eastern Europe or were descended from people who had immigrated from there at some point.

This was the time of the Red Scare. People like Senator Joseph McCarthy held hearings in Washington trying to ferret out communists in the State Department, the Army, and just about everywhere in government, publishing, and the entertainment industry. Many people lost their livelihoods during the paranoid frenzy of those times as blacklisting became commonplace. In my own family it was whispered that Uncle Julius had lost his job with the State

Department because he had been accused of having communist leanings. (It was actually simpler than that. Someone in the family once told me that Uncle Julius had a Black girlfriend and that didn't sit well with his superiors, so they found a way to get rid of him.)

I remember conversations in my home that were filled with fear. Most of my family on my mother's side were of Ukrainian descent. My father's side of the family were descended from those German folks who worked for Tsarist Russia until they were, one way or another, expelled from there. Many of them immigrated to America where they became known as Germans from Russia. None of my relatives had anything to do with communism, but as Eastern Europeans and Germans from Russia they were worried that they would, mostly because they were Jews, be somehow scapegoated. These were not unreasonable fears from a Jewish perspective. It was more unreasonable to them that they would *not* be blamed for something.

Rumors were spreading that the Jews were a part of the communist threat, and there was a palpable fear in the community that the next act of vandalism or violence could happen anytime and anywhere. Nobody felt secure. It was only a little more than a decade after the catastrophe of World War II and the killing of the six million. All of that was fresh in the memories of most people, and particularly Jewish people.

The night that the HUAC hearings were announced in the paper, some people came and destroyed Mr. Kaplan's fruit market. The windows were broken, fruit was scattered on the street and sidewalk, and all the display units were smashed and broken. There was nothing left. On a wall inside the store and on the sidewalk outside someone had painted the words "Commie Jew" in bright red paint. All the Jews in the neighborhood were devastated by what had happened. Devastated, but not surprised. As far as I remember, no one was ever apprehended and prosecuted for this act of vandalism, which was akin to terrorism. But all was not lost.

While many of the stores in the neighborhood were owned by Jews, many of the Italian men in the neighborhood were tradespeople.

Mr. Levine and Me

That day a half dozen pickup trucks arrived at the corner of Legion Avenue and Scranton Street. Men who were carpenters and painters cleaned up all the debris and loaded it up in a couple of the pickups. Others unloaded materials, lumber and everything that was needed to bring the fruit store back to life. Someone from a glass company came and replaced the broken store windows. In a couple days the store was back to doing what it did, selling fruit. Mr. Kaplan was very grateful and very happy. The whole neighborhood was grateful and happy. We had all experienced the evil of the vandals and the love of the carpenters.

I never knew the people who spread all that goodness. I wish I had. I believe they would have been great friends. But they were just a bunch of Italian men trying to do the right thing for a Jewish shopkeeper. Mr. Kaplan was not their brother. He was something just as, or maybe more, important. He was their neighbor.

Keeping Kosher

One day back in the 1990s, Rabbi Yael showed up at my office. I'd never met him before. He was a young Orthodox rabbi from Chicago who came to Lincoln two or three times a year to check on the kosher certification of a few businesses. One of them was Lincoln Snack Foods, which manufactured something called Screaming Yellow Zonkers, and another was the Martha Gooch flour mill. There was a third company he certified but I can't remember its name. Rabbi Yael worked for the Union of Orthodox Rabbis and part of his job was to see that food processors that wanted to be able to display the 'OU' symbol on their products were abiding by all the myriad rules that assured their products were indeed kosher. Many products carry this label, and those Jewish people who keep kosher rely on the OU and other organizations like it to help them to be sure that the foods entering their homes meet the strict standards they felt religiously obligated to follow. Rabbi Yael told me that since he had to come to Lincoln fairly often, he wanted to get to know the rabbis in town so he'd have a place to visit between appointments. There was only one other rabbi in Lincoln, the leader of the Conservative synagogue. I was serving the Reform congregation.

Each time after that first visit with Rabbi Yael, I made sure to have some kind of kosher nosh to go along with the coffee I always had brewing. Entenmann's danish was what I usually got when I knew he would be coming. We'd sit and talk about this or that for an hour or so in between his appointments, and I wouldn't see him again for maybe five or six months. He was an interesting person and I enjoyed visiting with him. Sometimes we'd talk about some text of Torah or Talmud, and other times about our families or what was going on in the news. I looked forward to hearing that Yael would be coming to town.

After a couple of years I realized Rabbi Yael visited with me but not with the rabbi of the Conservative synagogue when he came to town. This seemed a little odd to me. My way of doing Judaism was very different from Yael's. The Conservative rabbi followed pretty much the same religious patterns Yael followed, while I and my congregation felt free to modify practices and rituals. We were not very strict about the dietary restrictions, and we celebrated one day of Holy Days and festivals rather than the two days celebrated by the Orthodox and Conservative wings of Judaism. Head coverings were mandatory among the Orthodox and optional in Reform settings. We believed that Torah was the creation of people; Orthodoxy taught it was composed by God. Even the word 'God' was treated differently in our traditions. Out of respect, Orthodox folks spelled it 'G-d.' I could go on. The differences between our faith structures were many and touched upon almost every aspect of our religious understanding and lives.

Once when Rabbi Yael was in town and visiting with me I asked him, over coffee (and Entenmann's, of course), why it was that he always visited with me when he came to recertify the three food-processing companies. Surely he had more in common with the Conservative rabbi than with me. He thought about it for a minute. I could almost see the answer to my question forming in the expression on his face. Finally he said he thought I was wrong. He thought he had more in common with me. I didn't understand how that could be, given what I've written above. He went on and clarified what he meant.

"Michael," he said, you're right that we see our faith differently from one another. I have a point of view rooted in the long-standing traditions of Orthodox Judaism. You have a point of view rooted in the long-standing traditions of Reform Judaism. My point of view is consistent. So is yours. That consistency is far more important than any differences of interpretation we might have. The Conservative movement is sometimes as Orthodox as me, and sometimes as liberal as you. That, to me, is not consistent."

When Rabbi Yael left my office that day to head over to the flour mill, I thought about what he had said. Checking out that flour mill meant almost nothing to me and almost everything to him. I realized that he was right and I was right, even as we approached things with a different point of view. Our respect for one another, and reinforcing that respect from time to time is, I think, the best form of keeping kosher.

Honorary Italian

Before I began my seminary studies I was living in a rented basement apartment in a small town in New Jersey just off the turnpike. I had a job nearby in the anodizing department of an aluminum company and it was a convenient and nice place to live. The people who owned the house, Dominick and Maria, lived upstairs. They were great people: friendly, kind, and considerate, even loving. They seemed to me almost like parents.

The town, like many places in New Jersey, was home to lots of Italian people. I became friendly with some of them. Mr. Collura owned the diner in town and I went there pretty often, especially on the weekends. I bought wine at a shop owned by another Italian man, and I loved the little bakery where those wonderful Italian cookies could be had. It was Maria who taught me how to make braciole, that delectable, rolled flank steak stuffed with prosciutto, Pecorino Romano cheese, garlic, basil, and parsley, and sometimes boiled eggs, long simmered in a hearty tomato sauce. I make it sometimes to this day and when I do, I always remember Maria. She's part of my kitchen somehow, just like my grandmother Sophie.

One of the people I met while living there was Carmen. He was an insurance agent who sold life insurance for Met Life. His wife and business partner, Alicia, sold health and property coverage. Once I had gotten to know them, and knowing they were Italians, I invited them over for dinner and served a simple meal of chicken Parmesan with *spaghetti aglio e olio*, salad, and Italian red table wine. Dessert was cookies from the bakery in town and little cups of espresso I made in my stovetop Bialetti espresso maker. I still have that gadget and it still serves me well after all these years. I think Carmen and Alicia were impressed with dinner. There were no leftovers. They helped me to clean up before dessert and we took the cookies and coffee to the living room.

When Carmen and Alicia were finished complimenting me too much about dinner, Carmen asked if I would do a favor. I told him I would if I could and he told me his club, Americans of Italian Descent, or AID, was trying to raise money to help bring a child from Naples to Boston Children's Hospital for some exotic surgery. I told him I'd be happy to donate but he said he didn't need a donation from me. Instead, he said that he thought it would be great if I could make an Italian dinner for a few of the members of AID. They would sell tickets and maybe raise quite a bit that way. An Italian dinner for Italian people cooked by a Jewish guy. It sounded like a good but really daunting idea. He said he thought the dinner would be for maybe eight or ten, and I thought I could easily handle that. I agreed to do it. The dinner was set to take place a month later. Carmen told me I would be able to use the big kitchen at the club's building and that would be easier than doing it at home.

About a week before the fundraiser I called Carmen to ask about the dinner. He told me he had a couple members lined up to set the tables and to handle the cleanup. He said they had managed to sell some tickets, and he was happy about that. So, because I needed to know, I asked, "How many people am I cooking for?" Carmen answered, "I've got good news and bad news for you. The good news is that the tickets sold for fifty dollars each. The bad news...?" I could almost hear him grinning. "The bad news is, you'll be cooking for forty-five. We raised over two grand!"

He was excited. I was scared. I knew I was a good cook, but dinner for forty-five? So I told Carmen, "I guess I'd better get busy."

I had some vacation time built up and when I went to the aluminum factory that afternoon for work (I was on the three-to-eleven shift), I explained to my foreman what was going on and asked if I could take the week of the dinner off. He disappeared into the office and a little later he found me on the production floor as I was dipping a big rack of aluminum into an acid bath. He told me I could have the week off and I was glad about that. It put me at ease, and the thought went through my mind that my foreman must have been Italian. I'm pretty sure that may have helped with my request for vacation time.

When the week of the dinner arrived I made up lists of the tasks I would need to do. Then I created a menu. *Pollo alla parmigiana, involtini di melanzane, pasta aglio e olio, insalata,* wine, desserts, and coffee. Then I made up grocery lists and went off to start gathering what I needed. I was able to find just about everything at a supermarket. I went to Collura's and Mr. Collura told me he'd donate a big container of Spumoni ice cream. The bakery told me they would provide trays of their wonderful Italian cookies and loaves of Italian bread. The wine shop donated a couple cases of Chianti in their pear-shaped, wicker-covered bottles. I was ready to go.

An interesting sidelight to all this was that Dominick, my landlord, friend, and father figure, was the current president of AID. He asked me a few times how things were going but he didn't try to influence what I was doing. He gave me a key to the AID building so I could get in and out anytime I needed to do so.

Dominick came to America having been an Italian prisoner of war (POW) during World War II. His wife, Maria, had been a nurse at his POW camp, which is where they met. They fell in love and after the war they were married. Dominick was allowed to remain in the United States. He went to night school and after a while he became a citizen. He spoke of that with great pride.

I spent most of the day before the dinner in the kitchen at the AID clubhouse. I felt grateful that it was well equipped with commercial ranges, ovens, and appliances. There were all the utensils I needed, and importantly good knives and a sharpening stone. I pounded and breaded the chicken cutlets, fried them lightly, got them in baking pans along with a little of the marinara sauce I'd made early that morning, topped them with grated Parmesan and shredded mozzarella, and put them in the refrigerator, ready for baking later. Then I peeled and sliced the eggplant and made up the rollatini with

Keeping Kosher

prosciutto, Italian parsley, and ricotta. Those also went into baking pans with a little bit of a different sauce, chunky with tomatoes, bell pepper, onion, and garlic. I got the loaves of bread ready with garlic butter for baking later and chatted with the people who had come to help set the tables.

Right about then, someone from a local florist, Italian owned of course, came in with beautiful floral arrangements for each table. They placed the vases in the center of each table, gave me a hug, told me the place smelled great and said they'd see me later. I was just about ready. All I had left to do was fill a couple of gigantic pots with water and get them hot. I was going to need about six pounds of pasta to feed everyone. I also minced about half a dozen heads of garlic that I'd later sauté in olive oil and red pepper flakes. That would be the sauce for the spaghetti.

Dinner started. I had everything ready. Volunteers from the club helped out with the plating. Others served as waiters. Everything turned out well. When it was time for dessert and the tables had been cleared, Carmen went to the front and told the people how much money they had raised. He told them that I had donated the groceries, and mentioned Collura's, the bakery, the wine shop, and the florist. He told the crowd to give me a hand, and they did. I felt honored. Then Dominick got up and waved everyone silent. He said, "I don't understand it. You're Jewish and you cook like an Italian." Everyone laughed and applauded. Then Dominick said, "Migeleuch, come over here." He put his arm around my shoulders and drew me close to him. He picked up a frame from his table and held it up for all to see. It had the name of the club, the date, and some words about the event on it. And beneath all of that "Michael Weisser - Migeleuch, Honorary Italian."

I think that certificate meant more to me than the honorary doctorate I received many years later. Dominick, Maria, Carmen, Alicia, and everyone in the room were and are the kinds of friends scattered through the pages of this book and the spaces in my mind.

Thirty-Minute Friends - Epilogue

I began to write this little book at the suggestion of my daughter Debbie and her friend and colleague Steven Harrison. It happened in the accidental way things happen sometimes.

A couple months ago I was planning to drive from my home in Elmira, New York, out to Lincoln, Nebraska, for a visit with my son and daughter who live there with their families. I was looking forward to seeing all of them and spending time with them. Living so far away prevents me from doing that very often but I'm still game for a long drive across the country. It's worth it to be able to be with them for a while.

While I was in the midst of planning for my trip, getting a neighbor's son to cut my acre of grass while I was gone, finding someone to pick up my mail and water my house plants, I thought it would be nice if I could see my other daughter and her son also. So I called her and gave her the dates I planned to be in Lincoln and asked her if she could come to Lincoln from where she lived in Fort Collins, Colorado. She was not going to be able to do that for a number of good reasons. But my daughter had a great idea, one so clear and simple that I wondered why I hadn't thought of it myself. She said, during that call, "Why don't you spend the week in Lincoln and then come out to Colorado for a while."

I'm retired, a man without a schedule, so I agreed. A day or two later Debbie called and told me she could arrange for a place where

Thirty-Minute Friends - Epilogue

I could stay in Boulder when I came out. She worked with someone (it turned out to be Steven) who had plenty of room, and she thought I'd be more comfortable there. I agreed when she told me she would be in Boulder just about every day and on the couple of days she couldn't be there I could wander around and enjoy the beauty of the place.

I drove to Lincoln, about twelve hundred miles in two days, and spent a nice week visiting with family and friends. It was a very good time for me. Then I headed out to Boulder. When I got there Steven welcomed me to his house, told me I had the run of the place, and made me feel most welcome and comfortable and glad to be there. Debbie, true to her word, was there just about every day. We spent a good bit of time having the kinds of talks that dads and daughters probably should always be having but seldom do. It was not only a special time, but also, in some ways, a cathartic time as well. I think Debbie and I got to know each other more fully during that time in Boulder than ever before.

At the same time I was glad I had met Steven. He's a good person, exuding a spirit of peacefulness. I enjoyed getting to know him. After a day or two I offered to cook for us, and for the rest of the week I prepared different foods, holubtsi (Ukrainian-style stuffed cabbage rolls), meatballs and marinara sauce, chicken Parmesan, and a few other things. Steven called me the resident chef during a dialogue group gathering that met at his home now and then. He also called me the "wonder rabbi," but that's another story.

One evening Steven and I were having a conversation, a schmooze really, over dinner, and I told him that when I lived in New York and rode the 7 train between Manhattan and Queens, I'd often strike up a conversation with whomever was seated next to me. We'd chat until one of us got off the train, sometimes for the half hour it took to get from Queens to Times Square. I mentioned somewhere in that conversation that I thought of the people I met on the train, people I would almost certainly never see again, as thirty-minute friends. Steven told me that would be a good title for a book and that I should think about writing such a book. That chance conversation was the genesis for the book you're now reading.

There are a few words I say to myself as I begin to meditate each day: "I breathe in. I breathe out. Thoughts arise. I notice them. I don't follow them. I breathe in. I breathe out." As I wrote this book, I took a different approach. When thoughts arose, I did follow them. Even so, the writing was like a meditation. I started out without a real plan. I just started writing, my fingers on autopilot, as they typed out whatever I was thinking. If some phrase reminded me of another story I would pause, make a one-line note as a reminder, and go on with what I'd been writing. Little by little many thoughts arose, many memories emerged from their hiding places, and some of them found their way onto these pages.

If I had unlimited time to explore my memories, I think hundreds or thousands more stories might come to light. But here is one more that I think brings the thirty-minute-friend experience to life.

I used to walk down Main Street in Flushing, New York, nearly every day. It was a jumble of Asian grocery stores and restaurants. Most of the people on the streets were Chinese or Vietnamese or other varieties of Asian. Signs written in Chinese were everywhere. It reminded me, in an oblique way, of an earlier time known to me from history books of the old Lower East Side of Manhattan, which had been a center of Jewish life in New York. Throngs of Jewish people, signage printed in Yiddish, hustling and bustling, busy. The milieu was the same; only the faces and languages and aromas were different.

This is the way of the big city. One group settles in for a time and then moves on to greener pastures as it is replaced by another group. The faces change, languages change, signage changes, culture morphs from one model to another. And life goes on. But with all the changes it somehow remains the same.

After a while, the feeling of being an outsider, a stranger, faded away for me. The sights and smells became familiar, a few words of Chinese became part of my common vocabulary, and I became a part of the newness and oldness of the place. I started to recognize the faces of some of the strangers I passed on the street, or of clerks working in the multitude of little shops that were crammed together throughout the neighborhood. People became more and more real for me, and I began to notice more about some of them. Even if I didn't know their names or anything about their back stories, they became important to certain moments in my journey.

On Main Street there was a pizza shop. It was stuck between a Chinese grocery and a Chinese gift shop. All the other businesses were Asian, run by Asian people. The pizza shop stood out because it was one of the last remnants of a time that had passed. I walked by there every time I got off the 7 train and made my way down Main Street.

Several times each week I noticed a man with no legs sitting on a little wheeled square of wood. He had a sign propped against the wall beside him. It read, "I'm a Viet Nam Vet. I'll appreciate your help." On the sidewalk there was a plastic container into which people had dropped a few coins or dollar bills. Sometimes I would drop a dollar or two, or even a five, and then go on my way, feeling good about myself.

One day as I was walking by I made eye contact with that unfortunate "Viet Nam Vet" and I felt compelled to stop and speak with him. We talked for maybe half an hour. He told me the VA had pretty much let him down. And I told him that I had noticed him quite a few times. We chatted about this and that and then it was time for me to move on. So I dropped some money into his container and wished him well. He stopped me and said thanks. Then he said something I've remembered ever since.

"You're the first person who has ever spoken with me while I'm sitting here," he said. "It's more important than the money. You made me feel human."

I'm not the only one with these strings of random memories jumping across the billions of synapses in my brain. You have them as well, and I know for sure that every once in a while one or many

Mr. Levine and Me

somehow come from wherever they have been living into the light of your consciousness.
It's part of what makes us feel human.
Maybe you might want to share them sometime.

About the Author

Rabbi Michael Weisser

Rabbi Michael Weisser was a spiritual leader renowned for his profound compassion and transformative approach to confronting hatred.

Born in 1941 in New Haven, Connecticut, he overcame a challenging childhood to dedicate his life to building interfaith harmony and fostering understanding. Weisser's life was a testament to his unwavering belief in the power of love over hate, grounded in the Jewish principle to "love your neighbor as yourself."

A graduate of Hebrew Union College with honors, he served Congregation B'nai Jeshurun (South Street Temple) in Lincoln, Nebraska, for more than 20 years, first as Cantor and later as Rabbi. He also shared his wisdom by teaching courses on religion and spirituality at Nebraska Wesleyan University. Rabbi Weisser leaves behind a legacy of resilience, faith, and the enduring power of love to bridge divides and heal communities.